Leading with Obeya

"New ways of visual working has emerged considerably in the last few years. Obeya is a philosophy that can help you to understand how you can benefit from a visual language in your day to day business work. Visual thinking and doing is here to stay. *Leading With Obeya* is an engaging read to making the transition from traditional to visual management possible."

Patrick van der Pijl – CEO Business Models Inc., speaker, author of *Design a Better Business and Business Model Shift*, producer of *Business Model Generation*

...

"Keeping an overview and the ability to steer when it gets big and complex in fast and dynamic environments, how do you do that? Obeya offers a solution and its practical value has been fully demonstrated in recent years. But how do you set up a good Obeya and how do you effectively introduce this tool into an organization? With his book *Leading With Obeya*, Tim Wiegel has succeeded in creating a book that offers many answers, but above all shows giant practical experience. The examples provide guidance, the approach gives direction, and the setup is super practical. In short: highly recommended!"

Rini van Solingen – speaker, professor at Delft University of Technology and author of *How to Lead Self-Managing Teams, Formula X, The Power of Scrum, Scrum for Managers* and *The Responsive Enterprise*

"I read *Leading With Obeya* with a feeling of great anticipation because, whilst many people are aware of the literal translation of Obeya (at its simplest 'Great room'), few understand the philosophy behind its true use. I was therefore fascinated to learn how Tim would approach the topic and he didn't disappoint. Right from the foreword Tim confronts the paradigms of how you, and your organization, works and challenges you to think differently on every page.

What I really like about the book is that Tim doesn't expect you to agree with his every point, he simply wants you to think about how you and your organization needs to change to be successful, using the principles of *Leading With Obeya* to emphasize the importance of great Leadership. He uses some fantastic visuals and examples to engage the reader and he maintains an interesting narrative throughout.

The more people that are encouraged to move from a traditional management style to Lean leadership, the better, and Tim's maiden book will help you and your organization to make the change."

Philip Holt –Senior Vice President - Operational Excellence at GKN Aerospace and author of *The Simplicity of Lean* and *Leading with Lean*

Cover design and lay-out: Jorine Zegwaard, jorinezegwaard.nl

Editing: Dorseda de Block

Illustrations: Koen de Keersmaecker, Bizzuals.com

© 2020 Tim Wiegel & Boom uitgevers Amsterdam

Management Impact is a division of Boom uitgevers Amsterdam

ISBN 978 94 6276 332 6

e-ISBN 978 94 6276 396 8

www.leadingwithobeya.com

www.ObeyaCoaching.com

For Mieke and Lise

Table of contents

Part IV:

What's on the walls – five visual areas, eight hours a week

Part V:

Getting started - Transforming your leadership system

Appendices

Foreword

This book is about leading organizations using Obeya, which, if used well, helps maximize human leadership potential. In recognizing our human flaws, we're all willing, but not always able to do what's necessary to realize our dreams with an organization. I truly believe that leading with Obeya — a big room in which we visualize our work in relation to our goals, catering to our cognitive abilities — maximizes our human potential to help organizations on their quest to glory. I hope, in particular, those organizations whose quest is related to making this world a bit of a better place will be inspired to increase their impact because of this book.

Speaking of glory, who has seen much of it in their organization lately? I've seen many organizations embark on Lean or Agile transformation journeys, improvement programs, or stay with the status quo. But with the exception of just a few, none of them had major success in terms of successfully transforming the way they work and the way they think — at least not while I was there. Maybe I bring bad luck. Or maybe something else was going on.

I've seen organizations and management teams struggling with seemingly similar problems; I wonder if you might recognize a few of them:
- Meaningless strategic planning sessions and follow-up documentation that ends up gathering dust on the intranet.
- Trying to push a hundred projects simultaneously and nothing gets done.
- Getting stuck in firefighting mode as a result of "operational debt" (fixing your structural problems).
- Long, stale management meetings that seem to add little value, and everybody knows it.
- Administrative burden from reports that nobody seems to read.
- Siloed departments that barely cooperate or even communicate.
- Increased KPI steering by senior management in an attempt to gain control over what's happening in the organization.
- Stating people are the most important asset, but no one actually experiences it that way.
- Adopting and transforming new ways of working, like Agile from the outside, but sticking to the old habits from the inside.
- And so on...

I do hear stories about overcoming these typical issues from teams or departments that achieve major successes, but they seem to be very rare. In fact, they seem to be so rare that when they do occur, news travels fast and a lot of other companies start to try to copy whatever happened there and paste it onto their own organization. Take the Lean tools we've tried to copy from Toyota, the Scrum methods we tried to copy from Nokia, the squads and tribes model we've tried to copy from Spotify, or the OKR approach we're trying to copy from Google. But, like with real copies, whenever you copy something the quality just isn't the same, and on some copies, the ink tends to completely disappear after a while.

When I evaluate organizations and their approach to making things better and I set out to achieve their goals, it often comes down to a change program that focuses on operational teams, adheres to some new and sometimes hyped form or way of working, and is ultimately driven by the need to either make more money or spend less money. But since we can't describe it that way, we'll tell people we're looking for things like "agility." I've seen some pretty agile teams indeed, all scattered going in different directions but never the same. Unfortunately, that doesn't really help achieve the financial goals either.

I was never really lucky enough to come across an organization in person that, from work floor to top management, decided to do things radically different. The Dutch home-care organization Buurtzorg comes to mind, Semco comes to mind... and now we find ourselves back at naming a handful of companies that deliver major successes that others are trying to copy (and are failing in the process).

And here I am writing a book for you with a name in the title that probably fits your definition of a new hype. So why bother with reading about Obeya, after reading my perhaps somewhat cynical foreword this far? Well, lucky for me, Obeya isn't anything new, it's been around since the mid-90s, so technically I'm not sure we can call it a hype.

But using Obeya, or a big room with visuals, will not add any value unless you put the principles into practice. Those principles are easy to trace back to an origin well before I was born (1981). They are pretty straightforward and you will nod in recognition looking at them, but possibly go back to doing your work like you always did without displaying any sign of changed behavior. So no hype there either, but rather a question: what's holding us back to simply start applying a set of principles and ways of working that make complete sense?

The bottom line of this book is not to create a new hype; it is not going to magically shift your operational teams into high performance mode and it will not increase your earnings before the quarter is over. This book will help you reflect on the way we tend to lead our organizations. It will address some very powerful ideas that have been passed down from the last century and are still being adopted and refreshed in today's business literature.

You'll recognize a lot of these ideas in approaches like Lean, DevOps or Agile. The thing is, we haven't been really successful at providing leadership teams with an approach that helps them put these principles into practice. Leadership training and books are usually big picture regarding principles for behavior and such. Principles are great, but we're prisoners of our own habits. We read books, hear stories, and try to follow up on tips from a coach, but even though we logically concur those are good ideas, if they lack a practical way of implementing them in our daily routines, we think about them once or twice and then go back to doing what we always did.

The change that matters and brings about better organizational results cannot be cast upon your organization like a spell. Better and more affordable healthcare, more sustainable housing, higher profit margins, better engineered cars that wipe out the competition won't happen because you launch a program to "fix" the way your company operates. Results don't simply appear when your management team gets inspired on a leadership retreat. Your teams won't work faster if you hire more people. Your quality won't go up by bringing in more Quality Assurance experts. Your teams won't become more agile by hiring more Agile coaches. Your leadership team won't become an instant team of winners because you decorate a room and call it an Obeya.

If there's one thing I've learned from the successful teams I've been so fortunate to witness in person, it is the following: You will only achieve your organization's goals if you are able to establish dedicated, coherent, structured leadership that is devoted to nurturing teams and developing people Into an army of continuous improvers. You must provide them with meaningful work and enable them to grow and thrive in delivering value for customers and achieving your organization's goals. You will find testimonies in the stories and comments of the people I've interviewed in this book.

This book is as much about leadership as it is about creating a big room. If you don't change the look, feel and taste of your game on the leadership level you will keep getting what you've always got. If you're not looking to change your game you've probably wasted your money buying this book. But if you are ready to change, please read on. ☺

Finding stuff in this book

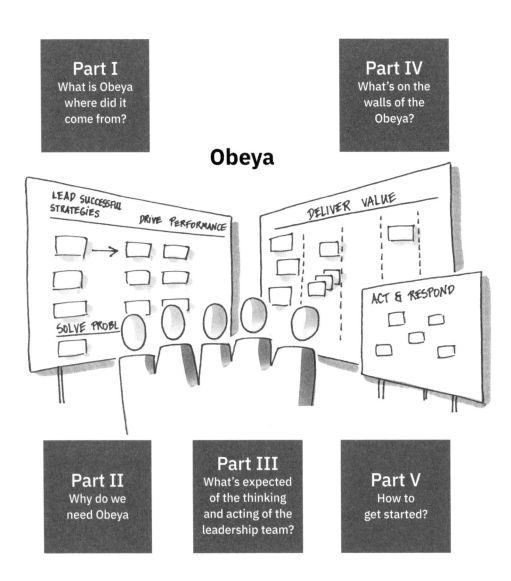

Part I
What is Obeya where did it come from?

Part IV
What's on the walls of the Obeya?

Obeya

Part II
Why do we need Obeya

Part III
What's expected of the thinking and acting of the leadership team?

Part V
How to get started?

Part I:
Introducing Obeya and the Leadership Reference Model

This book is for people interested in the development of (their) leadership capabilities in any industry or type of organization. If you are looking to achieve your purpose and achieve your strategic goals through meaningful activities on a daily basis, here is a good place to start.

Though the underlying principles in this book are inspired by Lean* and Agile thinking, our practical approach to explaining them allows you to take the first steps with an Obeya, even if you don't have a history with Lean or Agile.

But first things first...

What is Obeya?

The word Obeya means "big room" in the Japanese language. Why the Japanese connection? Because that's where the first "Obeya" originated, at Toyota when building the Prius.

The Obeya functions as a forum for leadership and operational teams to openly, visibly and respectfully engage to make the realization of the organizations strategy part of their day-to-day work. If done well it helps keep out ego-centered politics, confusing prioritization, malfunctioning management practices, misalignment, lack of direction for self-organizing teams and many other types of "traditional management issues."

WHAT WE CAN LEARN FROM A PRIUS

Toyota put Obeya into practice in 1993 when launching the Prius. Whether you think the car is beautiful or not, Toyota was able to deliver the Prius in about half the time to market compared to many of its competitors, and it became the leading hybrid car in the world. It's challenge was to double the fuel efficiency of a normal car at the time. The Obeya was setup as the central hub where the team would collaborate over the development of the car.

As Jeff Liker explains in *The Toyota Way* (2003) about how the Obeya was setup by the Chief Engineer (senior leader) of the Prius project, Takeshi Uchiyamada: "One

---

*   Lean, as used in this book, can be attributed to Toyota, as lead by the Toyoda family and refers to the works of authors like Ohno, Womack and Jones, Shook, Rother and others that describe the workings of the Toyota Production System (TPS) in terms of why and how it is successful.

of the personifications of the chief engineer is that they know everything, so even when developing different parts of the vehicle you know where the bolts can go together as well as what the customer wants. In the old vehicle development system, the chief engineer traveled about, meeting with people as needed to coordinate the program."

The challenge of the Prius was that it had impossible deadlines and a product that was significantly different than other cars they built. There was simply no time to do it in the old-fashioned way. The team needed to do more in less time and still fulfill the promise of quality that Toyota stands for. "So what could Uchiyamada do, since he did not 'know everything?' He surrounded himself with a cross-functional team of experts and relied on them. For the Prius, Uchiyamada gathered a group of experts in the 'big room' to review the progress of the program and discuss key decisions."

Figure 1.1 – Obeya and the Prius, sharing 360 degree context including mechanics and marketing

All the essential management information for the project was gathered in one area. There was one view, one version of the truth of the system to develop and build the Prius, to bring it to the market on time and with double the fuel efficiency.

Workers and managers of different disciplines shared their views of the product and performance visually in one room, creating a strong and meaningful context together. The cross-functional team was seeing, learning and acting together. By working with the prototype car and customer input all in one place, they enabled a focus on customer value and a comprehensive shared understanding with the team on the product to be delivered.

Toyota applied visual management in the context of the Prius project with a focus on the best approach for developing a product. It was an explorative journey, building a totally new type of car in an impossible timeframe. A lot of problems needed to be solved for which there simply was no easy answer, but the team was working with an unprecedented effectiveness.

The Prius was unveiled two months before the intended deadline, which seemed impossible to meet when it was announced to the team, especially for something that had never been done before. Toyota "had met their promise of delivering double the fuel efficiency of a similar gasoline engine car. What's more, the price tag of ¥2.15 (about 20k USD) million was even lower than what the media had reported back in March."

Jeff Liker, author of *The Toyota Way*, explains "The Obeya system has become a standard part of Toyota's product development system for all vehicles, a fundamental innovation in cross-functional collaboration now copied around the world." Today, the Prius is not just the best-selling hybrid in the world; in Japan it's the best-selling car, period.

USING OBEYA TO LEAD AN ORGANIZATION

In this book you will find that we move beyond the concept of Obeya as merely an instrument for visual management and into the realm of leadership in organizations. The reason for this being that teams that transform their classical management activities into a way of working that centers around the Obeya, they go through much more of a change than merely putting visuals on the wall. The change takes place in how a team works, how they interact with their colleagues, when they meet, how they look at their work, their leadership system, how they coach, and many other things that you will find in this book. In potential, starting the journey of leading your organization with Obeya has the potential to be a transformation of the way you look at leadership. When we talk about Obeya for the remainder of this book, we talk about it in this wider context.

The teams using Obeya that I've worked with were not building a car. They were not able to inspect the quality of the seats or check how well the glove compartment fit or whether the sound was nice when the door was shut. In fact, many of these organizations were services organizations like banks, public services, telecom or broadcasting. As such, most of the people on the work floor were knowledge workers sitting behind desks with a computer screen. When there is a car prototype right there in the room, you can see it, touch it and feel it, but in the case of knowledge workers it is more difficult as there is no physical representation.

The teams I've helped get started with Obeya were leadership teams whose product was not a tangible car, but an intangible object: the achievement of their strategic goals with their operational teams. As such, the Obeya on a leadership level needs help developing strategy and directing efforts towards achieving a purpose almost as tangible as having a car in the middle of the room, you want to connect with what's happening in your organization. So, in essence, it is an Obeya for leading your organization. I must emphasize straightaway, it is not just for people in a leadership position, but for anyone who contributes towards achieving strategic goals, just as the Prius had a cross-functional team.

The type of information displayed in a Leadership Obeya is usually a representation of the goals (purpose) of the organization, a strategy including customer and stakeholder needs, followed by a definition and outline of how value is delivered and how the organization manages to improve its performance capabilities to deliver that value. Usually, the Obeya is divided into several areas that each have a rhythm and routine describing when and how it is used by the leadership team.

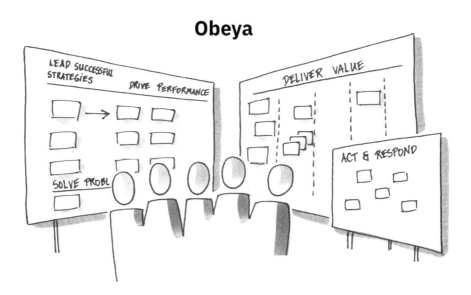

Figure 1.2 – Areas in an Obeya to lead an organization

You'll find many different layouts and setups of Obeyas. Every Obeya will look a bit different depending on who created it and where the team is in their journey (they will adjust the Obeya as they learn ways that work better for them). None is more "correct" than the other, but there are a few recommended ingredients we'll discuss in detail in Part IV.

Today, the concept of Obeya is being used by organizations around the globe. It has evolved beyond product development to cater to different types of organizations such as Boeing, Ford, Nike and ING Bank. The concept is being adopted by healthcare, industry, financial services and public services. It is a useful way of working for large, international companies, as well as for start-ups and particularly scale-ups, where context sharing is a common challenge.

Obeya was originally used to develop a product (car) in the context of a program. But when we use Obeya to support the leadership function of an organization, it has the potential to align strategy, sharpen focus, share meaningful context and bring about learning and improvement skills for both leadership and operational teams.

"The fixed rhythms providing set topics and meeting frequency provided us with clear purpose and agendas for each meeting. Especially the quick regular updates (15-minute meetings) on problems to be solved and need-to-know things were a big improvement compared to talking about a variety of elements and content that came up during a meeting. The weekly in-depth numbers update helped us create context faster than before when we were drip feeding them in different formats and moments during the week."

– Pauline van Brakel, Chief Product Officer

OBEYA ISN'T ABOUT THE VISUALS ALONE

Essentially, Obeya for leadership teams aims to unlock the full human leadership potential. The clue in using a visual management tool like Obeya is to cater to (the limitation of) our cognitive senses and introduce a way of working that forms new and desired behaviors through repetition and practice (Kata) to create new effective habits.

From here on we will talk about the use of Obeya in the form of a Leadership Obeya, and when we talk about the "team" it is the team that uses that particular Obeya to achieve their strategic goals. More often than not this is a team of people in a leadership position achieving strategic goals through connection with operational teams as well as senior management.

WHY USE OBEYA?

I've helped quite a few teams get started with Obeya, and a few months in they asked themselves, "How were we able to manage our organization before we had this?" There's something very powerful and very obvious in this way of working that really has the potential to change old leadership patterns, and changing behavioral patterns is exactly its strength.

> *"Two key benefits for us using Obeya: (1) the ability to make difficult trade-offs to optimize limited resources in support of the strategy, and (2) alignment by means of a framework that provides team focus on a common mission."*
>
> **– Fred Mathyssen, Senior Director**

Imagine a meeting where energy levels go up rather than down! Let's summarize a few of the benefits that can be expected when using Obeya:

Why use Obeya?

Better alignment between teams and alignment of purpose
With strategy, between teams, within the team
= more meaningful work

More effective meetings
Important stuff first, in the least possible time, clear accountabilities

Better insights & decision-making
Avoiding bias (as much as possible), using available (visual) context, facts & figures instead of assumptions

People development
Building leadership & improvement capabilities

Trust & collaboration
Transparency through visualization and dialogue creates trust in teams, up- and downstream

Rewarding
Effective change enabler
Visible results
Get rid of dusty boring traditional meetings

Figure 1.3 – Reasons for using Obeya

What you should know before you get started

THE CONTEXT IN WHICH OBEYA ORIGINATED

Obeya looks deceptively easy, but don't expect to be able to copy a trick and be effective at it. It is useful to understand the context in which Obeya originated to understand how it worked and why it worked then and there. Context tells us something about the way of thinking in which the idea originated and succeeded. Moreover, it will help you identify potential aspects that you might want to address in your own Obeya.

Obeya as a concept was first coined by Toyota, an organization already grounded in an improvement philosophy known for having successfully adopted the ideas and concepts of people like Kiichoro Toyoda, W. Edwards Deming, Kaoru Ishikawa and of course the "father" of the Toyota Production System as we know it today, Taiichi Ohno. Read their work and you will find an amazing amount of references to repackaged "modern" methods and ideas in the field of Lean, Agile and DevOps in various industries.

In this book we cannot presume to explain Lean or Agile principles and values properly as it would take several books to do so. But we can make a summary for you of the relevant thinking that plays a big role in the Obeya. This summary is far from perfect, but it should help you review whether this is being applied in your Obeya, and if it's not whether that's a positive or a negative.

I do recommend further study of Lean and Agile to increase your team's ability to achieve more results with (and perhaps even regardless of) Obeya in your organization:

- *Toyota Production System* (Ohno, 1978);
- *Lean Thinking* (Womack & Jones, 1998);
- *The Toyota Way* (Liker, 2004);
- Agile manifesto (Agilemanifesto.org, 2001);
- *DevOps Handbook* (Kim, Humble, Debois & Willis, 2011);
- *Toyota Kata* (Rother, 2009) and
- *The Triumph of Classical Management Over Lean Management* (Emiliani, 2018).

Lean & Agile elements in Obeya

Constancy of purpose:	Respect for people:	Pull:	Continuous improvement:
• Long-term goal setting & deployment • Identify customer value • Strategy visibly aligned on all levels	• Human interaction over processes & tools • Develop exceptional people , • Develop Craftsmanship • Relentless reflection • Leaders are teachers • Facts & knowledge are where the work is done	• Match supply with demand • Deliver in the smallest, earliest way possible • Just In Time • First Time Right • Minimum Viable Products • Respond to change	• Visualise systems to expose, inspect & solve problems, • Maximize flow, • Improve iteratively, • Autonomation • Verify hypotheses, scientific approach

Figure 1.4 – Listing some of the most important Lean & Agile elements to look for in the Obeya

In the Obeya, we will be looking for application of these principles. Do not be deceived by the simple appearance of these concepts. They are, in fact, incredibly hard to execute in practice in a consistent, qualitative manner so that they deliver results. Also, if the team is not willing to apply these principles at least to some extent, you end up applying a tool in a context that lacks the qualities with which it was once successful.

Fortunately, the ultimate goal of these principles is not simply to be able to apply Obeya, but to create the conditions for a successful organization. Many of the Obeya principles are ground in common sense, and the Obeya serves as an instrument to help you put them into practice through its visuals, rhythm and routines.

Jeff Sutherland, one of the founding fathers of Scrum (a way to adopt Agile in software development), said "Scrum is a way to implement Lean in building software. In fact, it has the advantage that if you follow it closely and implement well, you will be doing Lean as articulated by Mary and Tom Poppendieck without even understanding Lean." I'd like to think the same goes for using Obeya. If you use it well, you will be applying a lot of the principles mentioned here from a leadership perspective.

TIP - To see if your team is applying these principles look for visible clues and evidence in your Obeya during session (behavior) or on the walls (visuals). Example questions you could ask:

1. Can we see the strategic goals and how the things we contribute to them?
2. Are we actually exposing problems that are on our path of achieving those goals, or do they remain hidden?
3. Are we trying to achieve the goals, or are we trying to improve our system?

ARE YOU READY TO SHIFT YOUR PARADIGM?

Toyota has been very successful in creating a systematic way of working, growing their culture of continuous improvement and encouraging respect for people. Slowly but steadily they have taken over the automotive industry since the Second World War, overtaking leading global players like General Motors and Volkswagen.

"It can be very difficult to convince leadership of this way of working, and align them on one standard method to define and monitor strategy and performance."

– Fred Mathyssen, Senior Director

Obeya originates from that context and it is useful to understand what is expected from leadership style in an Obeya. Mind you, the style that we're looking for in an Obeya completely fits with the very latest (and earliest) management literature, from Covey to Mintzberg and Deming to Sinek. Here are a few style differences we expect to see in traditional management behavior and behavior that is based on Lean leadership principles and desirable in the Obeya:

Traditional management	Leadership in the Obeya
As a leader I must know all the answers.	As a leader I must discover the things I don't know in order to start knowing them.
Red is bad, we want only green.	Red means we understand where our problems and opportunities to improve are. If we're seeing only green we're not capable of exposing problems which means we're not able to get better at what we do.
Telling people the solution.	Coaching people to develop their capabilities to find the solution themselves.
We celebrate the one firefighter in the team.	Everybody must be able to solve problems structurally.
At the first sign of trouble we start shooting solutions from the hip.	Spending time to understand the root cause before talking about solutions, so we can make smart decisions.
The truth is in the Excel sheet.	The truth is where the work happens.
We reward achieving short-term objectives.	We reward sustainable improvements in the system that help us achieve long-term objectives.

Table 1.1 – Differences between traditional management and leadership in the Obeya

Do not expect to be able to setup and use an effective Obeya while holding on to a traditional style of management behavior. Just like teams have to make a serious change when adopting different ways of working like Scrum, so it is now the time for management to adjust. Managers who embark on an Obeya journey do well to inform themselves on what is expected of them, to avoid disappointment.

Moving away from traditional management ways and improving our behavior is a never ending process; there isn't a final "maturity level," in fact, mature leaders will recognize there is always room for improvement. Asking a coach to reflect on behavior or setting up peer-review sessions is likely a necessity, if only to address our bias driven tendency to overestimate ourselves or the challenge to recognize our own flaws.

Many teams, if they feel they need to improve their game, first start addressing their culture. They might do an assessment, coloring their team personalities or writing down their values, and later sign a charter to promise they'll abide by those values and agreements and use them in their daily practice. They might even primarily look at the culture of the operational team rather than at their own leadership level when it comes to options for improvement.

However, over and over we are learning that change doesn't happen by thinking about change, it happens by actually changing the way we do things on a daily basis. As some say "we can't think our way into a new way of acting, but we can act our way into a new way of thinking".

> **TIP** - While you read this book, keep in mind the change you might want to see in and with your team. What values and attitudes do you think need to change if you want to use Obeya successfully?

How does all of this relate to OKRs?

Objectives and Key Results (OKRs) is a practice that is being adopted by an increasing number of organizations today. You might have heard about or work with OKRs and might wonder how they relate to Obeya.

Just like Obeya, OKRs provide a system to set objectives, identify and monitor the achievement of key results. It does so through dialogue, engagement and alignment of employees in the organization in a cadence that suits the need for the ability to respond to change.

The Obeya is a great platform to support the use of OKRs and combine it with other relevant aspects of leading organizations. Using the Obeya as an instrument to visualize OKRs helps provide an overview of each persons' contribution towards the bigger picture. It also creates full transparency.

The Obeya encompasses objectives and key results and complements that information with necessary context for the leadership team to make decisions, solve problems and take necessary actions on a day to day basis. For example, next to goals and measurable results, we may also find structural problems, daily context, portfolio information and the actual flow of work on the walls of an Obeya. These are not just keeping us on the higher level strategic path (OKRs are recommended to review on a quarterly or monthly basis), but also help the leadership in the Obeya respond adequately to problems that need their attention today or tomorrow.

A big part of leading with Obeya addresses continuous improvement, which looks at a greater context than achieving a single objective. A potential pitfall with OKRs is that they originate from Management By Objectives (Lamonte & Niven, 2017).[4] As such if the people involved in setting the Objectives are not well trained, or lack insight into the full context of their organizational system (which is created in the Obeya), they might end up with promoting behavior that serves the individual, not the whole. More on this in Part II.

Obeya will supplement OKRs by addressing the full spectrum of leadership responsibilities and principles for thinking and acting.

Leading With Obeya - Reference model

Obeya for leadership teams helps by supporting the strengths and avoiding the weaknesses of human cognition and resulting decision-making. It is essentially the forum where people in your organization align, focus and grow their (part of the) organization towards achievement of the strategic goals.

The Leading With Obeya – Reference Model[*] purpose is to help identify the areas and principles that are the essential part in an Obeya for leading organizations. The

Reference Model has been developed based on Lean and Agile principles, values and learnings. It has been peer-reviewed by more than a dozen coaches from the field

---

[*] From now on we will refer to this as the Reference Model.

and by members of the Obeya Knowledge Network, applied in practice with several Obeya implementations for teams as well as used in trainings internationally.

The Reference Model provides transformation and development guidelines for a Leadership Obeya, to be used on any level in your organization. Every situation is different and there isn't a one-size fits all solution for what an Obeya must look like. What might work for an HR team in a commercial enterprise might not work for an operations department of an NGO. However, the key activities of the leadership team remain the same on a fundamental level. As such, the five activity areas and seven principles for thinking & acting remain relevant for any leadership team.

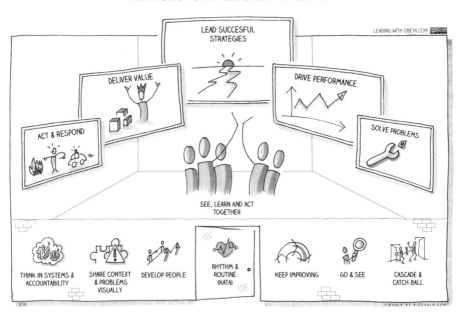

Figure 1.5 – Leading With Obeya – Reference Model

There are two types of aspects in the Reference Model, visible ones that you can see when you enter an Obeya and invisible ones that you will only see when looking at how the leadership team uses the Obeya. It is important to note that to make the Obeya work, all aspects must be represented, you cannot cherry pick. Even though you can start with just one area, you will find after a while that you're missing out on the others. My advice: do not call it an Obeya (yet) if you're just looking at a portfolio wall and haven't connected the dots with strategy, performance, problem solving, responding to daily reality and application of the related principles for behavior by the team.

VISUAL AREAS

Divided into five visible areas in the room, the leadership responsibilities describe key aspects of the work a leadership team should be doing. These parts will be explained in Part IV of this book.

PRINCIPLES FOR BEHAVIOR

These principles depict the way in which the team thinks & acts. The application of these principles will be visible when the leadership team uses the room and interacts with people, not necessarily just when looking at the walls. Since these principles play an important part in the creation of the physical Obeya as well as the start of the "transformation" process of the team, the principles will be explained in Part III of this book.

LEAD SUCCESFUL STRATEGIES	The starting point for any team, this area describes the purpose and goals of the organization. It lays the foundation for everything we do and defines the outline for everything else in the Obeya. **Example elements**: a purpose, strategic capabilities, customer & stakeholder analysis, market analysis.
DRIVE PERFORMANCE	Is our organization performing on the desired level so that we are able to achieve our goals? Can we test our business hypotheses? Should we pivot or persevere? What problems must we solve? These are the questions to be answered here. Example elements: metrics & indicators that help uncover and drive the performance of our organization.
DELIVER VALUE	This area displays the activities we are planning, to unfold the delivery of value to our customers. That means we expose our delivery system, make choices on how to best spend our limited capacity and communicate our plans with stakeholders. **Example elements**: a roadmap, portfolio funnel, value stream map, product backlog and strategic planning.
ACT & RESPOND	We've set out a course, but we don't know what's coming tomorrow. We need to be able to respond to change quickly and effectively. Teams must be supported and impediments must be resolved effectively. This way we can deal with whatever the future may throw at us. **Example elements**: Leadership Action Board, Inbox.
SOLVE PROBLEMS	In this area we use a structured problem solving method to make sure we remove the root causes of our organizational problems for good. As such we move from troubleshooting and fighting fires to improving our system sustainably. **Example elements**: Toyota Kata storyboards, improvement A3's, metrics.

Table 1.2 – Visual areas for the Obeya

VISUALISE SHARED CONTEXT & PROBLEMS	We must cater to the limitations of our brains, avoiding bias and assumptions. This is why we share context and expose problems visually, which greatly helps us arrive at better decisions and tackle complexity.
KEEP IMPROVING	In this area we use a structured problem solving method to make sure we remove the root causes of our organizational problems for good. As such we move from troubleshooting and fighting fires to improving our system sustainably. **Example elements**: Toyota Kata storyboards, improvement A3's, metrics.
GO & SEE	Instead of managing solely on the basis of reports, we regularly visit the work floor to provide support and challenge our assumptions. People on the work floor are the only ones that can show us how things really are.
THINK IN SYSTEMS & ACCOUNTABILITY	Instead of sub-optimizing a team or a part of the organization, we understand we must make the whole thing work if we want a better outcome for our customers and stakeholders. The accountability over our system is visualized and shows in our behavior.
DEVELOP PEOPLE	We respect people by educating them and nurturing their development. By investing in our people by teaching them coaching and improvement routines, we're building an army of capable workers, improvers and leaders that will make our organization thrive.
CASCADE & CONNECT	In our organization, each team is connected to the other, top-down and bottom-up, all the way through the value stream, and by people, not by email. In our interactions we make sure we understand what is needed and we reflect on our intentions to reinforce the effectiveness of our actions.
RHYTHM & ROUTINE	The only way to improve the way we behave as individuals and as teams is simply to start doing it. We use Kata to tune the heartbeat of our meetings and our routines to make sure we become super effective at making the right decisions at the right time, everywhere in the organization. If needed, problems go from work floor to top management in a day.

Table 1.3 – Principles for behavior

What does an Obeya look like?

Many of the pictures you'll find on Obeya on the Internet will show a display of a rectangular room that utilizes four walls to display certain categories of information. Reality is a bit different though, especially with lack of available rooms that have only four walls. The nicer Obeyas I saw all had windows and a fairly open vibe. The smallest Obeya could fit maybe eight people and the largest was constructed in two buildings in different countries and successfully facilitated meetings of up to thirty people (though that was far from ideal).

If you've never seen an Obeya and have no idea what it might look like then here are two examples to get a better picture in your mind. The areas of the Reference Model are mapped to each picture. If you want more detail of what's on the walls of an Obeya than is provided in the below pictures, skip to "Part IV: What's on the walls."

Example 1: Strategic program on a single wall

This Obeya was created for a strategic program. It has the strategy area on the left side, creating a horizontal structure for each Strategic Capability. Then there is the "Drive Performance" area with the metrics that translate the Strategic Capabilities into something measurable. Moving right, we see the "Deliver Value" area where milestones are assigned to each Strategic Capability. To the right of that is the area where problems are solved, and, finally, there is the "Act & Respond" area.

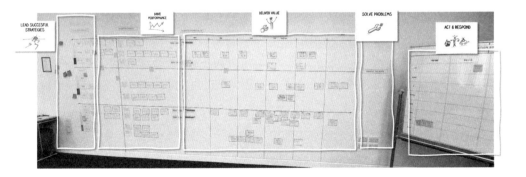

Figure 1.6 – Example Obeya for a program, left-to-right flow from strategy to actions

Example 2: Department using multiple walls

In this layout, we see the "Lead Successful Strategies" area define the Strategic Capabilities on the top, which flow down into "Driver Performance" with metrics. On the left, we find a number of improvement Kata storyboards that make up the "Solve Problems" area and to the left of that is the "Deliver Value" section. All the way to the right is "Act & Respond."

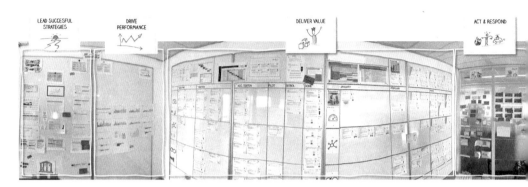

Figure 1.7 – Example Obeya for a department, top-down flow and various areas

Explaining what Obeya is without actually standing in one is very hard to do — and here you are reading about it in a book. Still, it is my intention to give you as much context as possible for a better understanding. So in addition to sharing pictures and drawings throughout the book, let's look at a practical application of the Obeya.

How does Obeya work in practice?

Fred Mathyssen, who was Senior Director of Global Operational Excellence at Nike, was so kind to share his story and explain how they got started with Obeya and expanded it over several locations in the world, including the US, Europe and China.

HOW DID YOU GET STARTED?

We got started with Obeya to simplify complexity. When you're in a leadership position in a highly complex international company, you've got requests coming from all directions. In the leadership functions I had it was always a struggle to simplify the complexity.

With Nike, we had many ongoing projects and too many metrics. The nature of the matrixed organization is that you will have multiple managers influence the priorities of a team or function. We couldn't easily tell whether we were working on the right stuff in support of the overall strategy. We needed to be sure we were working on the right priorities that would be in support of the corporate strategy as it cascades down through the organization.

When I first experimented with Obeya, I was responsible for a department called 'Lean Business Enablement' which was implementing various European projects focused on Finance, Supply Chain and Information Technology. Also within my responsibilities were the European Lean efforts, which made it easy to start an Obeya experiment that involved using a room for the first time.

We said "Let's figure out a way to get the most important projects up on the wall, including information on who's working on them and what the status is". The first step was to share that with the team. At that time I didn't even know it was called 'Obeya'. It was Steve Bell, who was lead coach at the Lean Business Enablement program at Nike HQ in Oregon and was also writing his book Lean IT during that period, who pointed out to me that there was a word for this type of room.

The team was very excited about this experiment. One of the team members explained it best by saying: "If it isn't in the Obeya, I'm not working on it", which was what it more or less came down to in terms of clarity and focus working with Obeya. It simply took less time for us to be on the same page and prioritize our work.

Seeing is believing with Obeya. When we had our Obeya up and running, people from over the campus would walk by and peek around the corner to see this room they had been hearing about.

Nike's CIO was so excited about this, he sponsored a video of our Obeya room, promoting this way of working as a benchmark for the rest of the organization. It soon became clear that this way of working was more impactful than we first anticipated with the experiment.

HOW DID YOU USE IT?

We evolved over time and created and expanded the Obeya concept. I was asked to lead the Technology Europe organization located at our headquarters in the Netherlands. It stretched my leadership skills because I had a very limited technology background. So without that knowledge, how do we get the team to be focused and work on the right things?

I quickly decided to use the Obeya as a means to lead the organization, which wasn't just doing projects but also delivering services. As such we built a room in which we realized an expanded use of the Obeya.

The approach was to first look back at the earlier experiment for learnings. Secondly, we decided to incorporate many more aspects of the over-all corporate, global and European strategy, allowing us to see the bigger picture on the wall.

It took us a few off-sites, refining all the information that we had gathered into meaningful insights in the Obeya. That was actually harder than we thought as we lived in the matrix, which meant that we had various VP's giving direction, many in-flight and newly requested projects, strict budgets, many metrics and a finite number of resources. But we kept developing the room, made mistakes but we continued improving!

The room was large and contained all the relevant information we needed for staff meetings, weekly, monthly and quarterly reviews and for project team working sessions. Our European GM would join us for a quarterly business review and there was no need for large PowerPoints... all the relevant information was in the Obeya.

We also held daily stand-ups with our own team to address the priority one tickets on the European level that were being handled by us. If there was a major problem reported, we'd use the room to address and track that problem. Almost everything we wanted to know during these meetings was on the wall, so why not use it?

Outside of the room there was a schedule of events for what meetings were being held in the Obeya. That helped us ensure the room was available during scheduled sessions but it also made it available for people wanting to have meetings and work with the information on the walls.

In the first Technology Obeya we had a room with a normal door which created more of a closed environment. So at some point we moved the Obeya to another location near the coffee corner and created a large opening with glass doors. Because of the openness of the room it stimulated the curiosity of our team and visitors promoting the sharing of information... a key component of an Obeya.

In the Obeya we had a metric on the wall which was people-related. The metric was very simple: "would you recommend a friend to work at Nike?". That metric could also be found at the departmental level at each of their walls. During the survey we'd ask anonymous feedback from people. This feedback was reviewed by management, corrective actions were defined and teams assigned. The details of this information were displayed in a common area and used during monthly employee meetings where status updates were provided.

This was actually an expansion from the Obeya just for this particular topic, we didn't do it for all the metrics in the Obeya. As leaders, we all take care that we're doing the right things for our employees. Communicating this back to our teammates was critical for us to show we were walking the talk: we're going to do something with their feedback. For example, we'd track and show our training program and speak openly about which teams were tracking to plan. The purpose was to ensure our employees would prioritize their development.

Figure 1.8 – Obeya room at Nike from the 2014 presentation

HOW DID YOU THEN GROW YOUR OBEYA TOWARDS OTHER AREAS IN THE ORGANIZATION?

At one point, we had one central Obeya for Nike Technology, which consisted of several departments, Infrastructure, Application Services, Portfolio Management, Business Integration, Functional Liaisons, and local tech teams in the countries.

So we built Obeya walls that resided at each department in support of running the actual day-to-day business in relation to the main Obeya.

Not all the implementations were equally successful. We learned that a key driver for a successful Obeya was the manager who was using it. One of our managers was fully opposed to the Obeya. But after a few months, he started seeing the clarity and focus that was created with Obeya and he turned a 180 degrees. His Obeya was always up-to-date and he actively used it with his team. Before there was the option of sifting through an unmanageable number of available reports, but you'd get lost in all the details. Now there is an area where the things that truly matter come together in one wall.

MOVING TO THE US

When I led the global operational excellence efforts, the focus was again more on the logistics and warehousing of our products. At one point, we had a challenge in one of our distribution centers. There was a lot of senior management interest from global headquarters to ensure we could ramp up the facility to its design capacity.

We were sitting in a small room with sticky notes all over the walls, trying to grasp the opportunities and prioritize our efforts. So I fell back on what I already knew to give us clarity, which was the Obeya. We prepared a presentation of what we'd need to set up the Obeya room. Once it was approved, we had the physical area built within just one week. Because we had the experience, we had done our homework and because there was leadership support, much was possible.

The local management team embraced the concept and that had a ripple effect on the other Distribution Centers as they were inspired by how we were working. There was a healthy competition between teams that were starting to build their own Obeya. Innovation and evolution in using Obeyas in your organization is a positive thing and can be facilitated through learning from each other's Obeyas. Learning is an important aspect to create synergy between the Obeyas too.

One of the challenges we had at that time was that there were so many projects that people were working on, that we couldn't do them all at the same time. We didn't want to throw it away, so we created what we called an 'opportunity pipeline' to ensure that we did not lose the great ideas that came from the workforce.

A strict governance model is necessary when running an Obeya. An example is the creation of a change control team. They would meet on a regular cadence and decide what work would be prioritized. The meeting was supported by the visuals we had in the room, like the opportunity pipeline, a value stream map, overviews of the teams, key metrics and all the executed projects.

At some point in this period we even started working with a third party logistics provider in our Obeya efforts. That was interesting because we basically expanded our way of working beyond the boundaries of the Nike organization. We started to see Obeyas being linked both within the organization and to our broader network.

OBEYA FOR SENIOR MANAGEMENT

There was a corporate need to standardize the way we looked at projects and metrics within our various distribution centers around the globe. Our vice president on his level essentially had the same need I had when starting with the first experiment: how to deal with all the complexity and how to make sure we have focus on what's important? If you have a set of global metrics that are then aligned from the top towards all these departments, there is much more consistency throughout. We also ended up building an Obeya for him.

It took some time to define metrics and start gathering them on a monthly basis. At first that took a lot of effort, but we made sure we improved the methods in which we did that so they became much more efficient. He was critical in helping define the top metrics needed to run the Supply Chain.

But building an Obeya on that level in the organization presented us with another challenge, because the amount of projects on that level that are running are just immense. Do you put them all on the wall? It wouldn't fit. Do you cherry pick? If you do, which ones would qualify? And if that's it and they represent only 60% of the total project budget, what do you do to manage the other 40%? We were having a lot of debates that revolved around the question 'what are we really building here'.

That's the art of it: how to figure out what you want to have on that wall. That art doesn't come by delegating tasks to everybody, but instead provide a direction and then dig into it with the team, make it work and improve it. It's a special skillset to be able to capture the essence of what you do and explain it and visualize it on the walls. And once it's there, you need to learn to have the right conversation that is as focused as the visuals on the wall. Just opening the discussion like in traditional meetings likely causes a lot of chatter but no meaningful, concise conversation.

In that discussion people need to feel comfortable reporting the "correct" status on their projects. That also requires building trust and it's a big responsibility of the senior leader. We can say 'problems are good', but not everybody will feel it that way. This takes time.

Observing the development of that room at the VP level, I realized how much I had learned from my earlier experiences, because I saw some of the pitfalls happening in that room. Because of the VP's global responsibility he didn't have the time to be on-site present with his team to work on a great room but needed to share his own vision on what he required. The VP would use the meetings in the room to be fully updated with the right information so he could then report to his superior. The Obeya helped figure out how to represent key relevant information to manage our warehouses around the world in a very practical and effective way."

Tips from Fred:
- Make sure your team owns the Obeya, they need to be engaged and feel ownership.
- Align your department efforts with the corporate, GEO and functional strategies.
- Get leadership on board and let them experience the value it provides.
- Don't get scared by the information on the wall, you can do it very efficiently, as also it replaces a lot of existing meetings, PowerPoints and reports.
- Learn to summarize the information, nobody wants to read lots of details.
- Invest effort into the governance model as it allows for crisp updates and course corrections when needed.
- Align your annual employee performance reviews to the Obeya as your team should be focused on and executing the department goals in support of the corporate strategy.

Part II:
Why Obeya is relevant for leading organizations

Before we move to the solution of using Obeya for leadership, we must understand the problem we're trying to solve, otherwise we might be tricked into pursuing wasteful action. Obeya is a very relevant and potent solution to your leadership challenges, but first we must understand why. So before we start designing your Obeya, let's make sure we're on the same page on the concepts of leadership and strategic management.

The leadership challenge

I believe there are three simple but essential tasks that anybody in a leadership position within an organization should be concerned with:
1. Establish the goal or purpose for the organization
2. Ensure efforts of teams and individuals in the organization are aligned towards achieving the goal
3. Facilitate teams and individuals so that they are effectively capable of achieving the goal

Essentially, the organization's strategy should encompass how leadership intends to fulfill these three tasks. But it doesn't appear to be as simple as it sounds.

Leaders[*] (which may refer to anybody in your organization), are, generally speaking, smart, hard-working individuals. They are responsible for achieving goals and the means to get there that matter to a lot of people either inside or outside their organization. They are expected to oversee difficult situations, make the best possible judgements and see to flawless executions of perfect decisions, or face scrutiny from their teams, peers, senior management, shareholders or stakeholders.

In order not to fail at any of this, leadership needs to be able to filter through the bombardment of information being fired at them at an almost constant rate in daily life through email, media, chat apps, big data reports, vast enterprise information systems and so on. Not an easy task—especially not when you live in an era where humans have never been exposed to so much information and where organizations have become vastly more complex since the start of the industrial revolution. Information technology, processing and offering evolve faster than humans can biologically keep up.

---

[*]   In this book when talking about leadership we address anybody in a leadership position regardless of the position of hierarchy.

So how to deal with all of this if you want to be the competent leader everybody is expecting you to be? How can you make sound strategic decisions when we cannot oversee the whole and look into the details at the same time?

Obviously the answer will be to use Obeya, but we're not quite there yet. Obeya is a means to help leadership execute their strategy in a succesful way. But since there is not one widely accepted definition of strategy, let's make sure we're on the same page there as well.

Obeya is a means to execute strategy, but what is strategy exactly?

The word "strategy" comes from ancient Greek, which is translated from strate-geos, meaning "Art of troop leader."[5] It stems from times where armies were commanded by leaders that were on a mission of conquest. It seems that human kind has been doing this forever, and today we still relate the word strategy to how we govern our organizations and lead them on a mission to fulfill a certain purpose.

To avoid making assumptions on this very widely defined but key topic of this book, we should define the art of a troop leader in a more modern and specific context. Here's a simple but effective one: Strategy is "the sum of all actions an organization intends to take to achieve its long-term goals."[6] This definition touches on three important points:

1. Intention means we actively investigate the best ways to achieve our goals through learning and careful study from our past and present experiences
2. Intention also means we can never know for sure what will happen and we'll have to prepare for reality to slap us in the face as we walk down the chosen path.
3. If strategy isn't translated into action, it isn't strategy, it just an idea.

Figure 2.1 – Strategy: from purpose to execution

Leading organizations is about developing meaningful, coherent activities with people in the organization while utilizing and allocating scarce resources in such a way that we can meet our (long-term) objectives.

TIP - Testing the effectiveness of your strategic leadership is simple. Write down the answer to these questions:
1. Which strategic goals must be met in order for your to be successful as a team or as an organization?
2. Do people on the work floor feel their actions contribute positively towards a purpose they are committed to?
3. Do your goals promote coherent action throughout the organization?

Did you answer the questions? How do you think others in your organization will answer? What if you walked over to an operational team right now and asked these questions, what answers would you expect to get?

HOW WE TRADITIONALLY 'IMPLEMENT' STRATEGY
One survey shows that in 2017 Strategic Planning was the primary tool used by management (Rigby & Bilodeau, 2018).[7] It starts with creating a strategic plan, of-

ten on an annual basis. Traditionally managers on each level of the organization are tasked with making sure a plan is delivered for the department.

Since strategic planning is an annual exercise, driven by the need for financial planning and accounting, it can be a rather non-inspiring administrative effort that simply has to be done to make sure budget is available for the coming year.

Before long, after the plans are reviewed and budget is allocated, the plan is communicated, shared in a presentation, perhaps a video message and a town hall. We go on managing the strategy based on reports that are reviewed on a monthly basis with red, amber and green status. Now we're back to business as usual, eagerly waiting to see the results of our efforts on the strategy.

Now, if all would go well, we would expect your organization is fully aligned, capable and effective at achieving its strategic goals, right? Employees come to work on a daily basis, feeling purpose in their work because they are part of contributing to something bigger. Teams and departments self-organize and align their efforts into coherent actions that maximize strategic value while delighting customers. Our time to market is reduced, profit margins go up, customers are more happy than ever and competitors are left miles behind. We rock at putting our strategy into practice!

THERE IS MORE TO STRATEGY THAN A PLAN

Somehow it doesn't seem to work this way. As Mike Tyson once said "Everybody has a plan until they get punched in the face." Though a direction for the future has been set by means of a plan, a few weeks into it reality catches up with us and we're back to managing the things that are right in front of us. Gone is the focus on the distant future and back are the problems of yesterday that we haven't managed to solve. For all too many business this is the reality of strategy execution.

The CEO feels powerless as she has no idea whether the strategy she just rolled out will be implemented successfully in the way it works, how its acted upon and if it will produce any results in the coming months. The only way to monitor progress is to set up metrics that are sifted from the work floor up through layers of management hierarchy. By the time the report gets to the top level, the world has changed.

In order to lead organizations, we must have the means to gather facts, test our strategic hypotheses and respond to new developments fast and in short cycles so we can pivot or persevere with our strategic choices. But on leadership level organizations tend to stick to classic meetings and (digital) reports.

MORE TEAMS, BIGGER CHALLENGE

The leadership challenge increases with the amount of teams you have. I once visited two Obeyas in a week that couldn't be further apart in terms of size of organization. One was a startup with three teams and the other was an international corporation with more than 15,000 employees. Where the leadership team at the start-up was able to closely interact with their teams on the work floor; get first-hand feedback on projects, progress and results; the leadership team at the big corporation was presented with tons of information that wasn't first, second or even third hand from the work floor.

Many interpretations and abstractions had been applied, and likely politics and bias in the process of making KPI and progress reports. That made me realize just how difficult it is to lead organizations if you're that far away from where the actual value of your organization is created and the strategy is truly executed (on the work floor). Without the means to create coherency and connection with the work floor throughout your organization, rolling out a strategy must feel like a daunting task. The troops are where the leader finds their true execution power.

SIGNS OF FAILING STRATEGY EXECUTION

In 1961 a now much recalled anecdote occurred when president Kennedy visited NASA for the first time and asked someone who was a janitor what he was doing. The janitor answered "I'm helping put a man on the moon!" That's a great example of a person who understands the purpose and has translated it to meaningful action.

One of the key tasks of leadership is to translate the purpose and goals of the organization into meaningful work for its employees. If done well, employee engagement will rise. But what is employee engagement? It can be defined as "the emotional commitment the employee has to the organization and its goals." (Kruse, 2012)[8] It refers to the intrinsic motivation of employees to care about their work and contribute to the organization's purpose and goals.

Why should we care about this? Many studies have proven employee engagement has a big impact on organizational performance. In a *Harvard Business Review* publication, Beck & Harter (2014)[9] suggest based on their research: "When a company raises employee engagement levels consistently across every business unit, every-thing gets better … including customer metrics; higher profitability, productivity, and quality (fewer defects); lower turnover; less absenteeism and shrinkage (i.e., theft); and fewer safety incidents."

In a small survey, we asked people questions relating to their leadership system (Wiegel, 2020)[10]. One of the goals was to see if the janitor was the exception or the rule. It turns out, almost 60 years later, purposeful activity on the work floor is not a common finding. A mere 48% of the respondents indicated their work could be linked to the strategic objectives.

Perhaps not surprisingly only 58% of respondents felt their job contributes to something useful. So if the art of the troop leader is to succeed in their mission, but the majority fails to see how they're contributing to it, and just a little short of half of the "army" feels they might not be doing useful work in the first place, how then would one expect to be successful?

Going to your job, finding yourself doing stuff but not knowing whether it will make a difference for anybody is tiring and even linked to burnout. It is suggested that: "To counter burnout, having a sense of purpose, having an impact on others, or feeling as if one is making the world a better place are all valuable. Often, meaningfulness can counteract the negative aspects of a job. Other motivators include autonomy as well as a good, hard challenge."(*Psychology Today*, 2020)[11]

Surely leaders spend a great deal of their time setting goals and making sure the organization is able to achieve them. But when asked, a mere 32% of the respon-dents of the survey indicated that leadership in their organization was spending the majority of time setting out strategic direction and facilitating teams in getting there. So what then is it that the troop leader is doing all day?

Probably, they find themselves struggling with issues that are typical for a lot of organizations. On the next page is a table with four categories of persistent man-agement problems. The table is a non-exhaustive indicative collection of symptoms based on my personal experience, supported by feedback from many people in my trainings and dialogues at organizations I've coached.

Goal Misalignment	No sense of priority or progress	Responsibility issues	'Primal management'
Competitive goals and KPI's between silos	Utilization is 120%, 100+ projects in the pipeline and nothing gets done	Firefighters are rewarded + promoted to leadership (and hire more firefighters)	Reactive, focus on short term (lagging, not leading)
Implementing tools and methods with no positive business outcome	Lack of system performance visibility (=unpredictable outcomes, no focus on improvements)	Lack of initiative and empowerment from front-line teams	"We're too busy to improve"
Annual top-down planning with no regard to workfloor realities	Progress on strategic objectives is ambiguous	Endless meetings with little added value and few meaningful actions	Increased top-down reporting load & micromanagement

Figure 2.2 – Typical problematic symptoms that make leading organizations difficult

So far everyone I've met has recognized these issues in their organization—at least if it was a mid- to large size organization. I believe there are four fundamental reasons why these problematic symptoms are so persistent when leading organizations:

1. Complexity of organizations.
2. Your brain (and everybody else's).
3. A century of failing management philosophy.
4. Neglect of the leadership system.

In the remainder of this chapter we will look at each of these reasons in more detail.

Reason 1: Complexity of organizations

Your organization, if it consists of more than a few teams, is probably a complex system. One way to recognize a complex system is that whenever you put something into it, there is no predictable outcome. For organizations that deliver services or products to customers, the input you provide is processed in the system, but there is a variability in terms of quality, cost or delivery (time) that is hard to predict by just any one person. The Leadership Systems Survey shows that, 94% of the respondents that are in an organization larger than ten people consider it to be a complex organization[12].

If we understand and improve just one piece of our system, there's no telling what it does on a systems level. Context, overview and insights into the mechanics of the system are needed: "Complex systems typically have a high degree of interconnectedness of tightly coupled components, and system-level behavior that cannot be explained merely in the terms of the behavior of the system components." (Kim, Humble, Debois & Willis, 2013)[13]. In other words, if you want better performance on an organizational level, teams and departments must get out of their silos and start looking at the bigger picture together, to oversee the battlefield and be able to make sound tactical decisions. By increasing common understanding of the system you increase your organization's ability to make changes and affect the organizational system's outcome in a positive way. It helps reduce complexity and improve predictability.

TIP - See if you can recognize any of these characteristics in your organization to determine if it is a complex system:
- Contains many interacting parts;
- Non-linear interactions;
- Contains feedback loops;
- Cause and effect intermingled;
- Can self-organize and adapt.

This last bullet might help explain why, even though attempts are made to introduce new models and trendy structures, your organization always seem to revert back to its old behavior.

COMPLEXITY MEANS YOUR INPUT AS A LEADER WILL NOT DICTATE THE OUTPUT

The problem with complexity is it doesn't bend or break by the rules of traditional management. Systems don't just do what you want because you want them to. A strategic plan alone is not enough. Deploying a strategy is a bit more challenging than just informing people of the direction you want to follow.

Throwing in a new org chart or team formation as part of a strategy through Agile or Lean transformations won't make a difference either. Culture follows structure is the basic premise for Larman's law[14] which suggests that unless the actual system is (re-)defined and implemented as a whole, without compromise, culture (the organizational values and behaviors) will self-preserve the status quo.

Stofberg (2016)[15] suggests that organizations, being organic in nature, should be managed like a "biotope": a natural ecosystem with a diversity of organisms, in which conditions are right for innovation to thrive. However a biotope doesn't listen to the orders of a CEO, so how do we manage for a desired outcome? Or can we manage at all?

Any leader with experience in sending strategic messages into the organization will know they have absolutely no guarantee it will change the organizational system, let alone achieve the desired goals. But somehow it seems we do treat our organizations this way. We are still learning that we cannot drive success in our organization mechanically as if we were fixing a washing machine, we have to learn how to change the behavior of living, non-mechanical beings (Taleb, 2012)[16].

There is no walking up to an ecosystem and telling it your goals and objectives, hoping it will respond and comply. You have to try to understand it, learn from it, respect its nature and then nurture and grow with it to achieve results. Nurturing a complex system requires commitment, sensing, probing, accepting that there is a lot we do not understand and a willingness to learn about it. You can accept complexity, and you must not neglect it.

Figure 2.3 – You don't fix a cat like you would a washing machine

Many things that are considered complex are hard to manage simply because we haven't spent enough time with our teams to try and understand the various elements and relationships in that complex system, and how it relates to what we want to achieve. This is the first thing we'll do when starting an Obeya.

Leaders need to learn to build relationships and alliances with other people in order to be successful. As such, they will need to drive performance through organic change (people, organizational, culture) as much as mechanical (processes, systems, machines, accounting structures) in addressing the complexity of the organization. You'll find that in the Obeya, human interaction is a key factor in dealing with this complexity as each person holds a piece of the puzzle of that complex system.

Reason 2: Your brain (and everybody else's)

We are more primitive creatures than we'd like to admit. Our brain has developed bit by bit over thousands of years into what it is today, and many of the behaviors we display on a daily basis are driven by parts of our brain that developed a long, long time ago. Sure, we have access to the frontal lobe which helps us make super smart, well-reasoned and intelligent considerations, but when put into modes of stress or anxiety we resort back to our more primitive ways of thinking and acting. If burn-out is an indicator of stress in the workplace, the fact that there is a 106% increase in cases of reported employee burn-out between 2006 and 2016 in the Netherlands[17] is likely not a good sign. Our primitive brains are working harder and sometimes too hard towards making as good as possible decisions in complex organizations.

THE BRAIN'S MANY ASPECTS

There are a few things we should know about how our brain works that are useful when viewed in the light of how people work in a (professional) environment. They explain why some things work and some things don't, and help us direct our efforts if we want to improve the way we interact and make (strategic) decisions to achieve our purpose.

Frontal lobe – associated with reward, attention, short-term memory tasks, planning, and motivation.

Temporal lobe – processing sensory input into derived meanings for the appropriate retention of visual memory, language comprehension, and emotion association.

Parietal Lobe – Activated when writing on a sticky note and placing it in an area of relevance. Also works when working with numbers.

Occipital Lobe – for visual interpretation and movement. For example, when scanning for triggers (e.g. impediments), or registering the movement of a milestone that is delayed.

Amygdala – processing of memory, decision-making and emotional responses (including fear, anxiety, and aggression).

Figure 2.4 – Areas in our brain at work during meetings at work

DOES BIAS AFFECT YOUR DECISIONS AS A LEADER?

Research shows managers make decisions "on the fly" with very little tendency to base those decisions on facts and figures that support those decisions[18] That shouldn't be a surprise. The primitive brain provides us with many useful and highly responsive pathways of thinking and acting. These biases have helped us on our evolutionary path, but also tend to bend our perceptions and decision-making towards impulsive reactions rather than conscious thought (Kahneman, 2006)[19]. There are more than one hundred fifty biases identified in the Cognitive Bias Codex (Benson, 2016)[20] that have a major impact on how you and I think and act every day, hour and minute. There are many that, when applied in a modern work environment, are likely to lead to unproductive thoughts and behaviors. Here are a few examples of pitfalls we might easily fall into if we're not conscious of our bias:

- **Jumping to conclusions**
  - o Attribution Bias – We see something in context and immediately apply certain attributes to it. For example, we are likely to think a beggar is a lazy person who doesn't want to study or work. We come to that conclusion much faster than we do to inquire about the real potential cause. The same goes for business problems, for example, when a sales pipeline turns dry it must be the sales people who are not doing their jobs properly. Or when our costs are too high we must lay off people because they are the highest cost factor for production.

  - o Confirmation bias – Once the first bias hits us we easily fall right into the next one, which makes us more susceptible to evidence or information that confirms what we've already conjured up as a conclusion. For example, if the CEO doesn't like the sales director because he doesn't agree with her policy, she might see declining sales pipeline figures as a confirmation that the sales director is not doing their his very well. And with that thought she's disregarding any other potential reasons, for example, competition has launched a newer, better product, or our own product quality has degraded. We are no longer objectively looking at what's in front of us, but rather strengthening the information that tells us we're right and weakening or disregarding the information that tells us we're wrong.

- **Firefighting/getting lost in daily operations**
  - o Delmore effect[21] – Makes us focus on smaller easier tasks that are less important but more easy to accomplish than the bigger (perhaps more strategic) tasks.

  - o Hyperbolic discounting[22] – If we can do something that rewards us shortly after the act, we prefer to do that over doing things that have a reward that lies far into the future. In fact, we discount rewards that are not immediate, giving a higher preference to the low hanging fruit. As such we're not working on the long-term strategy but rather the short-term wins, even if they do not contribute to the long-term goals.

- **Avoiding complexity**

  We tend to avoid complexity. Complexity takes time and a lot of processing power to tackle. In fact, one could say something is complex simply because we do not understand how it works, yet. As such we favor simple looking things over complex things, probably because we can deal with them more easily. As such, simpler problems are addressed rather than more complex ones.

- **Substitution of questions**

  We substitute difficult questions with easier ones (Kahneman, 2009)[23], for example, when we ask the project manager "how is your project going," the project manager is likely to reframe the question to "how do you feel about your project today?" Which is likely to produce a much more subjective answer than desired. We should avoid substitution of questions, which is why we carefully formulate questions in the routines of the Obeya, as you can see in Part IV.

- **We make choices based on what's good for ourselves (not necessarily for others)**

  We tend to make decisions based on our own interest. Though the outcome does support the egoistic need for self-gain, it is not necessarily something we do consciously[24] Various workings in our brains lead to making decisions that support self-interest or that make us more likely to support ideas of people or ideas we already favor. Hence, we want to make decisions in an environment where all members of the leadership team are on a level playing field, surrounded by objective information that highlights every important aspect of the system in which we make decisions.

- **Our brain makes things up**

  Our mind constructs things that aren't there, or tends to disregard information if it does not contribute to our predetermined goals. If we do not support our perceptive inputs with visual management and routines, our behavior will be highly influenced by our brain's attempt to interpret reality with minimum efforts, taking the shortcut rather than analyzing the intricate truths surrounding our (business) challenges. This means that if I'm a leader, I will make decisions that I believe are right, but do not necessarily help the greater good. Instead of learning and reflecting on what I thought would be good for the organization, I choose a direction based on what's already primed in my mind and I find or concoct evidence to proceed, while unconsciously ignoring signals or evidence that indicates the greater good is suffering from my actions.

- **Over-estimation and reluctance to learning**
  - o We tend to over-estimate our abilities, also in relation to other people's abilities. As such it is harder to admit our flaws, ask for help or learn from others. This is more so in western cultures than in the far east[25].

So that's a list of just a few things that happen to both you and me if we don't actively prevent ourselves from falling into the bias trap. But how do we avoid it?

ACCESSING YOUR CONSCIOUS BRAINPOWER

Kahneman (2009) suggests we have access to two systems of thinking which he simply (and consciously) calls System 1 and System 2. System 1 is our survival system – always on and extremely responsive, it helps us, for example, get out of situations of acute danger, say when we meet a bear in the woods. System 2 is much slower to kick in and we have limited access to it because it requires much more energy. We have to put it to work consciously, for example, when calculating a math challenge while doing a juggling exercise.

System 1	System 2
• Fast	• Slow
• Superficial	• Mindful
• Subconscious	• Conscious
• Short term	• Long term, big picture
• Survival	• Progress
• High availablity	• Limtied availability
• Energy saving	• HIgh energy usage

Figure 2.5 – System 1 & 2 thinking-properties

The challenge for organizations is when we need System 2 to solve complex problems, while we also need the consciousness to fire that system up in the first place. Many complex problems we face in organizations today are delivered under time pressure and often accompanied with extreme information overloads about the problem itself and also useless information and distractions. So we'll need a lot of System 2 to face the challenge of solving the complexity that surrounds the effective execution of strategy, but at the same time information overload and time constraints prevent us from activating that very system.

In the Obeya, the rhythm and routines help us free up time so we can engage our System 2. That means we have more System 2 availability to address complex problems, rather than focusing on the proceedings of the meeting itself.

Moreover, in the Obeya, we engage our brains more actively by using various stimuli consistently in relation to goals and facts. Rather than reading an email or a report, there is active engagement. People move around the room, pointing things out. There is not a speaker and an audience, or just two people at a table of eight that are actively engaged in the discussion. Instead, there is a life-size visual structure with facts and data, with people standing and actively engaging in answering questions that are essential to practicing the craft of leading organizations. Effectively, that means your brain is lighting up more synaptic activity than in the dusty old meetings that you're used to. (Attolico, 2018)[26] This creates more engagement, stronger memory and supports System 2 thinking.

How engaged and active is your brain?

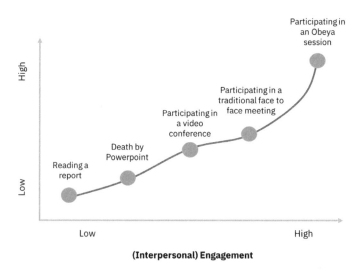

Figure 2.6 – (Slightly biased) indication of how different types of information sharing may affect your brain activity and engagement with other people, adapted from Attolico (2018)

Reason 3: A century of misapplied management philosophy

MANAGEMENT BY OBJECTIVES

In the 20th century, there have been a few major influencers of management philosophy. One of them was Peter Drucker, an economist that introduced "Management By Objectives" (MBO) to the world of management. It's a much-adopted system that is responsible for the way we do accounting and reporting in "Westernized" societies today. The philosophy is great, it's just that we're not fit to live up to its expectations.

The idea behind MBO is that a manager is evaluated based on the outcome of his work by measuring the achievement of objectives given to him or her. The basic underlying assumption is that any person who's a manager is smart and creative enough to make sure those results will be met. And if they don't, they're likely not fit for the job.

This kind of evaluation and system that promotes results is also applied in many school systems. If you don't meet your grades you'll fail and retake that year's class. As a result, there is a tendency to find ways to pass exams, like through training for the exam (rather than the acquisition of knowledge and skills), or by cheating. In essence, achievement of the objective is the only thing that matters.

If the outcome is a green status towards a given objective, we expect praise and reward. If the outcome is red a firm talk by whomever is your boss can be expected, if not more serious consequences. By fixing on achievement of KPIs while disregarding the evaluation of how that KPI is met, a lot can go wrong in terms of accountability in the process of achieving those results.

One persistent problem with the way we look at management is that the major qualifier for evaluating its success tends to be money. It is the only way we express value of a company and it tends to be the primary driver for incentives and this behavior. I have absolutely no issue with making money in fair, responsible ways. But if you want to foster a healthy organization that drives quality for its customers, you're better off not making money the primary driver for success, but rather the result of being successful (next to a bunch of other outcomes like customer satisfaction).

The brain's reward center is such a strong influencer of behavior that in setting personal Objectives people tend to:

a. focus on their own goals, forgetting the bigger picture to be successful as a whole, leading to siloed behavior in organizations, teams and people;

b. be driven by incentive salience[27], which keeps them working on objectives that have become obsolete or should be de-prioritized due to changed circumstances;

c. do whatever they can to meet the objective even though it includes doing things that are on the border of unethical or beyond;

d. hide problems that might indicate the failure to meet the objective in fear of punishment, signs of incompetence or

e. people tend to disconnect the pursuit of improvement once the objective is met, as there is no more reward in doing so, in fact it may raise the bar for next year's bonus which is undesirable as it will make the objective and related reward harder to reach.[28]

And all of this is OK, we're only human after all. You cannot blame anybody for pursuing rewards for themselves. But, you can start to think about reward (and, as such, motivation) in a different way. And I believe the world needs this, since there are plenty of examples of crises and scandals that have been driven by the blind and relentless pursuit of objectives. To name two of them:

• The mortgage crisis in 2008 – The objective was to make more money by selling mortgages. All figures were green, people were making loads of money, but the mortgage system was badly broken.

• The diesel scandal by Volkswagen in 2015 – The objective for building these cars was to meet the limits of the emission test, not to make cars that were actually cleaner.

A DIFFERENT VIEW ON WHERE TO FOCUS YOUR MANAGEMENT ATTENTION

Interestingly, there was another great influencer in the last century that disagreed with Drucker's Management By Objective. His name is W. Edwards Deming, who played a big part in promoting the continuous improvement cycle to Japanese car manufacturers in the 1950s. Deming explicitly disagreed with Drucker's view that performance increase comes from setting objectives and disregarding the system. According to Deming, the focus should be on the process that leads towards achieving objectives, and any objective should always be reviewed with respect to value for the customers and stakeholders.

Ironically, while Deming's message didn't seem to have significant impact in the Western management practices, it did land quite well in Japan. Indeed, studying the Toyota Production System (the foundation for Lean), one will find strong references and proof of practical application of Deming's view of continuous improvement in their way of working.

In the Obeya, meeting objectives is not the goal. Just like multi-year projects are impossible to plan, multi-year objectives are impossible to define in a future we do not yet understand. It is essential to understand the direction, the true north, and consistently focus and align our efforts on moving towards that direction. But not by predefining measurable outcome targets and neglecting their intentions with regards to the efforts of how they are achieved. The objective has become: continuous improvement, with respect for people.

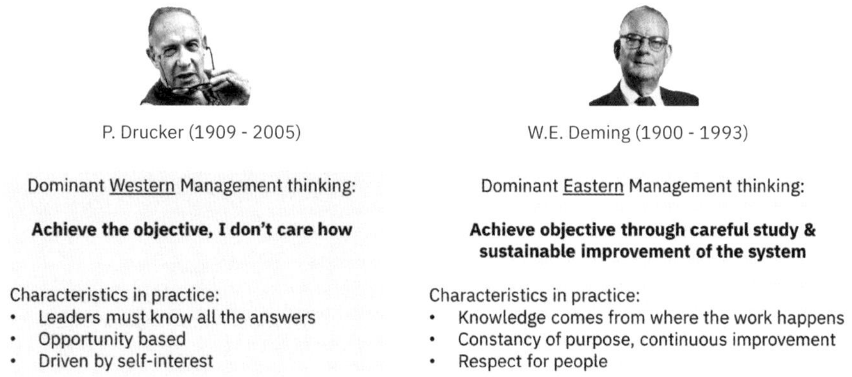

P. Drucker (1909 - 2005)

Dominant <u>Western</u> Management thinking:

Achieve the objective, I don't care how

Characteristics in practice:
- Leaders must know all the answers
- Opportunity based
- Driven by self-interest

W.E. Deming (1900 - 1993)

Dominant <u>Eastern</u> Management thinking:

Achieve objective through careful study & sustainable improvement of the system

Characteristics in practice:
- Knowledge comes from where the work happens
- Constancy of purpose, continuous improvement
- Respect for people

Figure 2.7 – Drucker and Deming's points of view were towards the same goal but with different ways to get there

We focus on improving the way we work while constantly monitoring our progress, setting new challenges, conducting experiments and reflecting with our (next in line) customers in order to achieve the desired strategic results. While we're at it, leaders will not only adopt this approach but will also mentor their team members to build a powerful and consistent learning capability in our organization that will then expand its strengths.

Teams that are successful in adopting Deming's view of performance improvement feel comfortable raising performance thresholds, causing reports to turn red instead of green. They are intrinsically motivated to improve the way they work and truly see a red signal as a guide that helps them focus on what they must improve. Gone are the days of watermelon reports*. Right? So what's holding us back?

HOW TO DEAL WITH OBJECTIVES AND METRICS IN THE OBEYA

Management By Objective is thought of as the cause for a lot of very persistent problems in the world we live in today. And that's not just because of the people who chase targets, but also how the targets were set and managed. A research on KPIs in sales context in 2008 (Franco-Santos & Bourne)[29] found ten common issues with target setting. It is important to note that the organizations in this research have, like many organizations, tied people's performance towards organizational KPIs to their bonuses and financial rewards. Deming once said "where there's fear, you get the wrong numbers." I'd like to add another one-liner to conclude the point of this chapter: "when there's money to be made, the system will be gamed."

Let's look at a few known objective-setting issues and how to deal with them in the Obeya. The objective setting issues in the below table are from the before-mentioned research by Franco-Santos & Bourne (2008), on the right we find the approach to these issues in the Obeya.

---

*   A watermelon report is one that is green on the outside, but red on the inside, meaning that even though the report reads green, the underlying performance is very poor.

Objective setting issue	How to deal with it in your Obeya
Target-setting was mainly based on past performance and soon perceived as too high or low by the people being assigned to that target with a bonus attached to it, because it would affect the feasibility of meeting that target.	There should be no relation between meeting targets in the Obeya and getting a personal bonus. This avoids behavior for personal gain at the cost of the team's efforts to get results on a systems level.
Targets were allocated inappropriately across the sales force.	Performance is a team effort in the Obeya; everybody supports the total outcome.
Some targets were based on the wrong performance measures - This was often referred to as "hitting the target and missing the point".	The metric is primarily meant to understand performance of the system, so it is for learning more than anything else. The point is to understand what must be done on a systems level to enable the achievement of our goals.
Targets were entirely based on financial indicators – even when factors such as customer relationships were absolutely critical.	In the Obeya, finance is just one of the metrics. The balance between all key success factors is monitored with financial aspects sitting on the same level with topics like customer satisfaction, employee happiness, and corporate social responsibility (depending on what your team chooses).
The data analysis process on which targets were based was poor and lacked rigor.	Through use of the continuous improvement pattern, metrics and targets are continuously reviewed and studied for their relevance towards impact on our system.
Targets were not periodically reviewed – so were overtaken by events.	In the Obeya, we look at performance and progress every two weeks on a systems level. Every meeting starts with potential changes to our plan or problems we encounter on the way to deal with them head-on.
Targets were "given" to people – so not creating ownership.	Goals formulated in the Obeya are cascaded from strategy and agreed in a handshake between people and teams. That always includes a statement by the person who will be working on any kind of target: "this is what I think we must do next, and this is what I need from you to do it."
The interrelation between targets was not considered – causing inconsistency.	In the Obeya, performance is looked at as a whole, balancing each key success factor with the other so we understand how each element is affected by the other.
Agreed action plans were the exception and not the norm.	The rhythm and routines incorporate regular sessions regarding performance to learn from actions and experiments that were taken, and the best next steps are considering what was learned from the results.

Table 2.1 – How to deal with objective setting in the Obeya

Reason 4: Neglect of the leadership system

"Any analysis of leadership that looks only at leaders is bound to fail."[30]

– Haslam, Reicher & Platow

WHAT IS A LEADERSHIP SYSTEM?

If we peer inside an organization and completely simplify the way we look at it, we see two kinds of people: one is busy thinking about long(er) term goals and trying to ensure we achieve them, and the other is doing work that is actually valuable to customers. Each has their own type of work and job description, processes and ways of working. As such, let's say there are two systems at work in the organization as a whole. And they are dependent on each other.

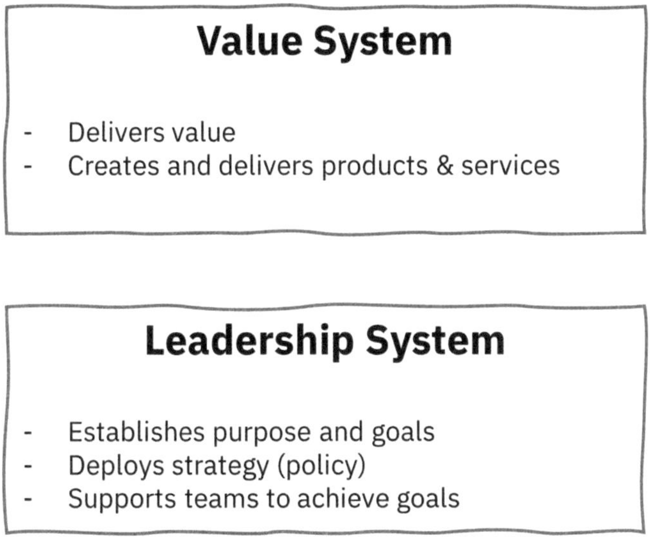

Value System

- Delivers value
- Creates and delivers products & services

Leadership System

- Establishes purpose and goals
- Deploys strategy (policy)
- Supports teams to achieve goals

Figure 2.8 – Leadership System and Value System

Value System*

This is where operational teams do "value-add" activities to create, deliver and/or provide products or services that are valuable to customers**. In the value system, patients are cured, bank accounts are opened for customers and cars are assembled so they can be used.

The idea of this system is to maximize valuable outcome for customers, ensuring that they get what they want, when they want it under the conditions they want it in. In the context of this book the value system also encompasses functions that either add value to the organization (e.g. promotion of products and services to increase profit), its employees (e.g. providing HR services) or stakeholders (e.g. accounting and regulatory reporting).

In a bike factory example, the production system is everything that happens on the work floor, both for products (e.g. bikes) and services (e.g. the website to place orders, selling the bikes).

Figure 2.9 – Leadership system and Value system in The Bike Factory

---

* People knowledgeable about the Toyota Production System will recognize this as the "Production System" but applied in a wider context to include services. The key narrative is that the actual value is created in this system.

** When we refer to "customers" it can be anybody who is receiving a product or service from your team, department or organization. Think of both paying customers, patients, users of public services, but potentially also other teams within your organization that are using the services or products that you've created.

Leadership System

The leadership system* provides the context, facilitation and fundament in which the Value System operates. It provides goals, sets policies that provide for the needs of stakeholders (e.g. government regulation or environmental targets) and creates an overlapping system that connects multiple products and/or services under the umbrella of the organization's purpose.

The Leadership system is ultimately responsible for ensuring a strategy is created and aligned with the Production Systems in such a way that the delivery of value is optimally matched with the utilization of the organizations limited resources in order to achieve the purpose in the best possible way. And that about sums up the key challenge for leadership.

WE LOOK AT THE SUCCESS OF LEADERS, NOT LEADERSHIP

Years ago I was on an assignment with my old colleague and friend Bart Stofberg to help a management team with defining their new strategy and operating model. One of the questions he suggested we used was "what is the definition of success for your team?" A seemingly straightforward question to which surely everybody has an answer, I thought at the time. After all, if this is not clear to us, then how do we agree on prioritization of our work, align with teams, or even show up to work every day?

I learned an important lesson from interviewing each individual team member. Some came up with an immediate answer, others took two or three sessions of one hour to come up with a suitable definition. But still, each person's view on "when are we successful" was different. I was amazed that such a seemingly simple question could be so difficult to answer and at the same time be answered so differently within a team that works together on a weekly basis. Few teams that I've met in the past 13 years truly had a common understanding of their own purpose and activities and how they relate to the overall organizational purpose.

---

*   "The term "leadership system" refers to how leadership is exercised, formally and informally, throughout the organization; it is the basis for and the way key decisions are made, communicated, and carried out. It includes structures and mechanisms for decision making; two-way communication; selection and development of leaders and managers; and reinforcement of values, ethical behavior, directions, and performance expectations." (Baldridge Glossary, 2019)

Figure 2.10 – Leaders focusing only on their own piece of the puzzle instead of looking at the whole

AUTONOMY WITHOUT ALIGNMENT LEADS TO CHAOS

If each team member exercises their leadership responsibility of aligning teams towards achieving a certain goal, and we're not really clear on what that goal is, then what does that do to our organization in terms of alignment?

In my interview with Fred Mathyssen, he called the phenomenon of a new manager introducing their own methods while disregarding existing methods "the flavor of the day." All the investments, projects, learning, etc. would be discarded.

But even when all managers stay put, the variety in both leadership styles by individuals, as well as their personal interpretation of goals, adds to complexity in our organizations. Interactions with one leader will lead to different results than the interactions with another leader. High variety in management priorities and behavior is not known to be an indicator for efficient, coherent action, particularly not if the function is supposed to provide coherence and alignment for the organization.

PROBLEMS WITH INDIVIDUALISTIC LEADERSHIP

If it's "every man and woman for themselves," what problems may we expect on a leadership level?

- Potential discontinuity in leadership quality – when leaders leave, the quality leaves with them.
- Lack of educating internal capability – no way of growing internal leadership qualities.
- Siloing – departments are driven by their own goals, not by common goals.
- Variability in quality – inconsistencies in approach.
- Waste in methods / ways of working – applying ways of working that are counterproductive for the other.
- Waste in alignment – we need more meetings and might be working on non-related projects instead of finishing a project together.
- Firefighting mode – instead of fixing the system structurally, we respond only to the problems within our own context.

Individualistic leadership

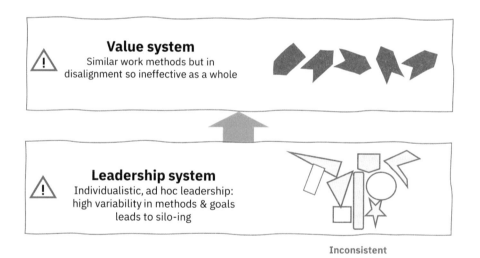

Figure 2.11 – Ad hoc leadership disrupts the value system

I once witnessed a "top-10" priority list that was: "the priorities, all on equal level." As such, true prioritizing work was left to the individual manager on the next levels of management. What made it especially difficult after that was that operational teams that were serving multiple customers were eventually left with the task of prioritizing the work. What happens when a team, that is supposed to deliver value to customers, is not facilitated by leadership and needs to spend additional time on organizing and facilitating alignment with other teams? Next to not being supported and facilitated by a leadership function, they also have to spend more time on non-value adding activities of alignment, reducing the available time to add value for customers.

We must find a way to translate our organizational goals systemically and coherently from purpose and strategy to meaningful work that engages people, in order for our organization to thrive. It is a leadership task, no matter where in the organization that leader is.* And we cannot leave it up to the individual leader to find their own best way to do it, as that provides absolutely no guarantee for organizational-wide success. We must look at it from a more systemic perspective and develop the skill of alignment with similar quality for all our leaders. But how do we make sure our leaders develop that skill?

HOW DO WE DEVELOP LEADERSHIP

A research by Gallup shows that 82% of the time managers were chosen because they happened to be very good in their previous, non-managerial position — so they have little to no managerial experience. How do we develop the qualities of a great manager? Moreover, how do we develop them to being a great manager for *our* organization?

Leadership is a craft a person can learn. It's a combination of skills, talent, plus the context of where and when that person leads a group of other people.[31]

It strikes me that in almost none of the organizations I've worked with so far was there a systemic, predictable, transferrable, coherent approach to how leadership teams learn to translate purpose into action with operational teams, and actually practice it and improve upon that practice.

Instead, we tend to promote people we like rather than people who help develop actual capabilities in the organization. Research has shown that in the model of Western leadership, managers with a higher chance of promotion are the ones that spend the most time on networking and the least time on development of people. (Judge & Robbins, 2013)[32]

---

*　　Self-governing teams have leaders in their unit, but still benefit greatly from a consistent model for alignment between teams.

Organizations seem to put individuals in a leadership position and then ask them to fulfill the bare minimum requirements through compulsory reporting for management and staff (risk, accounting, etc.) and management (progress, performance). The measure of success of that person is then defined by his or her ability to achieve the reporting objectives, often tied to personal targets. The rest is up to talent, often supplemented by generic leadership training.

Research shows managers are most rewarded for "achieving short term performance objectives," followed by either "knowing the right people (networking)," and "fixing acute problems or crises."[33]

The organizational system will not reward you for being a great manager, it will reward you for achieving your objectives and being a great firefighter.

START DEVELOPING THE LEADERSHIP SYSTEM, NOT JUST LEADERS

In one survey, 65% of the respondents disagreed that their leadership teams have set up their way of working in such a way that they can effectively facilitate and align with operational teams. Isn't the key function of the leadership system to ensure operational teams can get meaningful work done?

Systemizing the way you organize leadership in your organization not only makes it more efficient and effective, but as it becomes a consistent (repeatable) way of working you can now start training and growing people into that leadership system. It provides a context for teams that they can rely on and will function coherently throughout the organization. It can help you break out of the habit of firefighting on an individual level and start solving the real problems on a systemic level.

Additionally, if we have a standard for a consistent leadership way of working, that method can be taught and learned and improved upon through the chain of leadership as well as new aspiring leaders from the operational teams. In fact, it is a model to grow both people as well as your entire leadership capability. The Obeya is a great way of bringing standardization in your leadership system, while maximizing the utilization of your human leadership potential.

"The proof that our leadership system was working, showed in the fact that we were back at the desired levels of business performance faster and more visibly than other departments after reorganizations."

– Liedewij van der Scheer, Lean Black Belt

From here on, we'll start approaching leadership in organizations in a systematic perspective. Shifting the paradigm from the individual leader to looking at leadership as a whole is a necessity to improve the system. Aligning the purposeful parts with each other and the whole is necessary in order to reach a state where the overall purpose of the organization can be reached (Gharajedaghi, 2006)[34]

A leadership system serves operational teams* in optimizing the total efforts in the organization towards achieving the goals and purpose for the organization in the most effective way possible. In that sense it enables the execution of successful strategies.

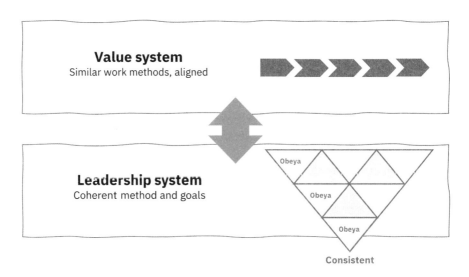

Systemic leadership

Figure 2.12 – From ad hoc to systemic leadership using Obeya for leadership teams as pieces of the puzzle

* Operational or operational teams are those teams that actually deliver value to customers and stakeholders, rather than fulfilling overhead management functions.

Obeya introduces a systemic approach that inherently requires next-in-line levels in the organization to be included, creating both consistency in management technique as well as unprecedented alignment towards a single purpose for all levels of management and operational teams in the organization. This gives meaning to everyday work, inspires people with ambitious targets and above all energizes your organization. Visible outcomes start pouring in thanks to higher developed learning and improvement capabilities across the board.

Strategy execution through all levels of the organization

The approach to creating a conscious connection between all levels of the organization is not new at all. Hoshin Kanri is a well-known concept for strategy management that finds its origins halfway in the last century in the Japanese roots of Quality Management (hence the Japanese name). The four components of the name nicely sum up what it aims to achieve (Hutchins, 2008): [35]

- Ho – means Direction.
- Shin – refers to Focus.
- Kan – refers to Alignment.
- Ri – means Reason.

Important aspects of Hoshin Kanri are to connect all levels of the organization both in terms of Direction and Focus (exercised through decision- or policymaking) as well as Alignment (through participative dialogue at each level or area of the organization with the next) and Reason to learn together and provide evidence of the effect of that strategic direction and learnings to pivot or persevere from the strategic path. You will find Obeya as described in this book relates to Hoshin Kanri and positions the Obeya as a practical means to make strategy execution part of the routine for leadership teams.

Part III:
Principles of seeing, learning and acting together

SEE, LEARN AND ACT
TOGETHER

Obeya can really help teams achieve their goals, but it can look deceptively easy. If you think the Obeya is all about the visuals, think again. Rather than the visuals, it is about you and me and how we interact in this room. The visuals are just there to support our cognitive abilities, it's how we act on them that matters most.

Let's see how Obeya can play a role in the development of your leadership team. Having worked specifically with Obeya for nearly a decade in different settings and branches, I find that using this instrument can have a profoundly positive impact on the effectiveness of leadership teams, both in terms of leading the organization towards a goal as well as day-to-day management tasks. Teams starting with Obeya consistently report the benefits. That's not because of what's on the walls, but because of how they're able to translate the essence of their work into something meaningful, visualize it, share it with each other and their teams, and put it into an effective work routine that has visible results.

"We're much more aware of what we're doing and what that means towards the strategy. Before everybody was busy one way or the other. Now, we have more focus on checking whether we've made the right progress towards our target and consciously make choices on whether we should launch a new initiative or not."

– Benjamin de Jong, Agile Coach

The key to its success is visible and even tangible representation of the otherwise obscured leadership system. Just walk into the room and you know exactly why the people in this team come to work every day, where they stand in terms of progress and how they intend to achieve higher performance in the future. Moreover, everything they do has a clear link to business strategy, creating focus on results. Whereas the team at Toyota working on their first Prius had the prototype of their car in the Obeya area, a leadership team in the Obeya makes the best possible effort to make their organization as tangible as that Prius prototype, through visualization and dialogue.

The only way to make this work is to make sure every aspect of the system of your organization is represented by people in the room who are willing to see, learn and act together. The team must embrace a way of thinking and acting towards uncovering the "Prius" of their organization. In the Reference Model, we find the aspects of thinking and acting in the Obeya in the walls or fundament in the bottom. In this chapter we'll discuss each one of them to understand how they contribute to seeing, learning and acting together. Lean and Agile practitioners will recognize these principles, though in this book we'll explain them in relation to the Obeya and from an initiate perspective.

Figure 3.1 – Principles for behavioral we expect to see in the Obeya to make it effective

One cannot judge the effectiveness of an Obeya by the visuals on the wall. They are only the tip of the iceberg. The majority of the mass is under the surface. Do not expect to start using an Obeya and get different results without changing habits and behaviors in your team. The real value is created through the behavior and decision-making of the team using it.

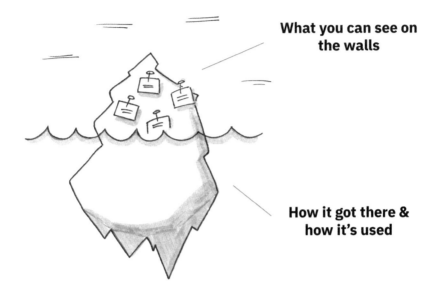

Figure 3.2 – Iceberg in relation to the visuals of the Obeya

The visuals on the wall of the Obeya are in fact a representation of how the leadership team understands their own leadership and production system. As such, certain ways of thinking and looking at the organization, people, products, etc. are exposed. What's on the walls is the result of what the team is willing and able to show about their work to each other and the rest of the organization.

The ability to create effective visuals in the Obeya is likely very different from the skills used in their "traditional" ways of management. The team must realize they will start a journey of practice and continuous improvement in order to get the most effectiveness out of their Obeya, both from a visual perspective and from the perspective of habits and ways of thinking.

We will now discuss the key concepts of thinking and acting that are the foundation for a leadership team's successful use of Obeya.

Systems thinking & Accountability

We've seen in Part I that due to its complexity, your organization likely does not have an input-output mechanism for executing strategy and achieving purpose. You cannot enter a command-line code and expect a successful delivery or outcome. Politics, siloing, personal targets (KPIs) and, frankly, the fact that we cannot predict the future and oversee how everything and everyone in our system will respond to change makes it hard to get to results in an effective way.

If we don't try to understand the system and how it affects decisions and actions that are taken on each level of the organization, it is likely that "luck" will have more of an effect on the outcome of strategic planning than "skill." That's why systems thinking is important: we must work together to expose and start understanding the system that our organization is.

DEAL WITH YOUR SYSTEM AND ITS COMPLEXITY BY EXPOSING IT

In his book *Antifragile* Taleb (2006)[36] talks about "causal opacity": We simply don't know exactly how complex systems work and how one thing relates to the other. We cannot predict exactly what will happen if we influence one specific aspect of it. Because of our bias towards complexity, we tend to avoid facing it head on to make sense of it. Instead we start poking around with "troubleshooting," whenever a problem (or more likely a symptom) occurs and mitigates it with a "patch" rather than a solution. But we simply don't see this happening because we can't see through the complexity of our system.

Another way of dealing with outcomes from the system that are undesirable and also not understood is applying more process and administrative burden. For example, if there is a problem with a product at the end of the production cycle, a frequent tendency is to add testing to prevent the bad products from reaching the customer. But testing can be tedious, time consuming and does not add any value for customers. In Lean ways of working, searching for the root cause helps expose more parts of the system and create an understanding of why the system produces quality issues in the first place. By removing that root cause, quality is raised and waste of material (faulty products) and valuable time is prevented.

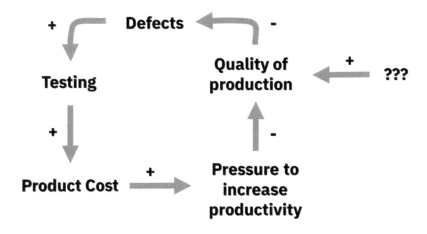

Figure 3.3 – In this loop, quality will go down and product costs will keep going up. Finding the system's root cause for poor quality is essential to break this cycle

But in order to do this, you need time. Patching up problems or symptoms appears to take less time and therefore feeds on System thinking. But in doing so we likely subject our already complex system to wasteful action, fixing the same symptoms in different ways all over again while covering up the root cause. Our System 1 thinking fails to see the possible negative (or positive) effects as a consequence of our fire & forget actions.

Example: The Bike Factory needs lower production costs

To understand your system and reduce the complexity of it, it is useful to spend some time creating a visual representation with your team. This is done through visualization techniques, for example, by making a causal loop diagram like in Figure 3.3, which can be used for sharing context with the other members of your leadership team.

Let's see what that could look like if we take an example. In the Netherlands, we love to ride our bike everywhere. Imagine you have an organization that manufactures bikes, The Bike Factory. Now this factory is discovering there is fierce competition from other bike builders. The challenge is to make high quality bikes that are affordable so they can compete with the other bike builders. We now have identified two (of potentially many) elements in our system: production cost and quality of the bikes.

That introduces the first friction point between two elements of your system: lowering costs by purchasing bike parts from suppliers that are cheaper, but that also tends to affect the quality of a bike when assembled. Perhaps we can find other ways of lowering costs without purchasing cheap but low quality bike parts.

Let's look for another element that might cause lower costs for bike production. Labor cost is one example that tends to be a significant part of the cost of manufacturing a bicycle. If we can find a way to reduce the labor cost per bike, then we can also keep the cumulative production cost of a bike low. Now there are two new elements in the system that we can uncover that affect labor cost per bike: wages and the number of bikes produced per cost unit (hour). So let's reduce the cost of labor. Soon we're finding out that our top bike engineers, those who manage to assemble the most bikes in one hour according to the right quality standards, are leaving because they can make more money elsewhere.

If that trend persists we enter a negative spiral. The quality and production of our assembled bikes drops. What part of the system can we influence in the system to create a positive effect?

What if we could increase the amount of bikes produced per cost unit (# of bikes / wages in € per hour)? That would mean more bikes with the same amount of wages so the average cost of producing a bike would be lowered. Perhaps can improve our process to find a way to build more high quality bikes with the same amount of people and wages. There you have a nice launching point for starting an improvement, to be discussed in "improve continuously."

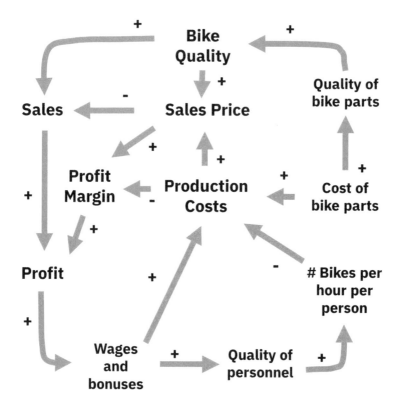

Figure 3.4 – Elements that might be useful for The Bike Factory to monitor in their Obeya in order to enter the competitive bike market

In this example, you'll find that at each step we uncover more parts of a system that are each related and have an effect on the other. If we want to lead this organization to glory, we must learn to press the right buttons in the system, rather than blindly setting the objective of lower cost. If we started lowering labor costs or costs for parts, we would no longer be able to fulfill our purpose, building high quality bikes that are affordable. Instead, we should inspect and respect the system and find the right buttons to press. But that button is usually not immediately visible; it is hidden beyond the immediate visibility of the system.

HOW DOES THIS WORK IN OBEYA?

In the Obeya, the system as the leadership understands it is visually represented by everything that is on the wall. In a sense, the visuals that are on the wall are the elements of the system that the team has been able to uncover and lift from the fog. The improvements that they are doing on complicated or complex problems in Solve Problems are related to those elements. And with each step they are taking into the fog, they are uncovering better understanding of that part of the system with every improvement cycle. And with that understanding comes better decision-making.

It should be mentioned that uncovering and understanding complex systems is a process of empirical research based on hypotheses (with the knowledge currently available to us we think this part affects that part, but we can't be certain yet) and gathering evidence, (turning this knob affects the other in a predictable way, indeed), and a healthy dose of humbly acknowledging that we know very little about how our organization really works.

> **TIP** - Creating a visual systems diagram of your system can be very useful for your leadership team to get a basic understanding of their system and share context. Beware, it is not an easy exercise. It requires time and mental focus by the participants and a capable facilitator who understands the principles of systems thinking[37] in order to get a useful outcome.
>
> Accepting that you'll never get a full grasp on a predictable system is useful. Do not expect to be able to control the system that is as complex as your organization. But you should indeed make efforts and use tools that will help nudge it in the right direction. That is an invariably better approach than looking at the elements of the system individually in reports on your laptop, hidden within departments and unexposed to the shared context and understanding of the team.

ACCOUNTABILITY IN THE SYSTEM

Why talk about accountability in relation to systems thinking? Think of the system as a puzzle. By uncovering the system's pieces of the puzzle, we start seeing the elements that should be managed by our organization. In order to be able to manage our organizational system, each element or piece of the puzzle should be represented by a person who is willing to take accountability for it. So when we put all pieces of the puzzle together as a system, each one of those pieces is represented by a person in the room. We now start seeing how the responsibilities and decisions of one person in the room (e.g. cost efficient operations in our bike factory) affect the other (e.g. bike quality). In Figure 3.4 we see various management disciplines operating as a system: HR hires and keeps high quality engineers, while Operations produces bikes efficiently and Procurement tries to buy cheaper parts.

Decisions of one person in the leadership are likely to affect others in the room. Some will be straightforward (using cheaper materials is likely to lower your production cost) whereas others are less obvious and indirectly related (cheaper products might lead to increased product returns because of poor quality).

In the Obeya, every element of the system should have at least someone who is responsible for the representation of that element. As such, when we start uncovering areas for improvement in the system, we are also able to come to an action holder quickly. As such, ambiguity around responsibility of performance by the system is defeated by uncovering the elements of the system and identifying the representative and accountable leader for each element.

Figure 3.5 – A person to take accountability for each part of the system

Share context & problems visually

A picture is worth more than a thousand words. We all know it, but do we act like it? Sitting at a table with thick reports on your lap is not a good way to support the brain. You will engage only part of it, make your management meeting boring (your brain is only partially active), and you'll also be prone to bias and assumptions driven by a lack of relevant and properly visualized (presented) information.

We don't visualize things in the Obeya because it looks cool, or plaster sticky notes against the wall because it fits with the latest Agile hype. Instead, we visualize the system and our work in the Obeya because our sight is our strongest sense (Witten & Knudsen, 2005)[38]. In fact, the visual cortex is the largest system in our brain[39].

Using PowerPoints for decision-making? That's great, but chances are they are built to support the outcome of a certain decision, rather than presenting your views in an objective way with the right level of information and the objective facts about the system and context of a problem. How many times have you had the feeling that the project manager's report was greener than it should have been in hindsight?

Figure 3.6 – Sharing context in done through dialogue

CREATING SHARED VISUAL CONTEXT, TOGETHER

The goal of visual management, essentially, is to cater to our cognitive visual abilities by helping us see the system and how effectively it is working, while trying to avoid bias.

As we've seen in "Think in Systems & Accountability," when we can look at the system as a whole we can learn more about how one area affects or relates to the other. We're able to spot the effects of deploying activities and test them against our assumptions of their contribution towards our strategy. We try to do this in the most objective way possible by agreeing on rules for when signals are used. For example if progress on the development of our new bike tire deviates more than 10% from the intended launch date, a red flag is raised on that topic, visually, on the walls.

If we think something matters or should matter to our leadership team, we should strengthen that through objective visual representation of the entire system. By selecting those things that matter most, and visualizing them in a neat, creative and meaningful way, we are actually building a stronger perception of our (understanding of the) system. Also, we make key information more accessible because it is on top of mind or available instantly at the place where we make our key decisions.

Since every piece of new information we receive during a day will shed new learning and new context on a subject, sharing context is a key activity for leaders to ensure their colleagues and teammates also receive that context. In doing so, they promote alignment and well-informed decision making everywhere, including outside the Obeya.

Research shows that managers who seek to share information and explain their decisions are more effective at what they do (Robbins & Judge, 2007).[40] Everybody has a piece of the puzzle and it's not until we start putting the puzzle together, and are able to see if the pieces fit that we can maximize the value that each individual is creating. The sum is greater than its individual parts.

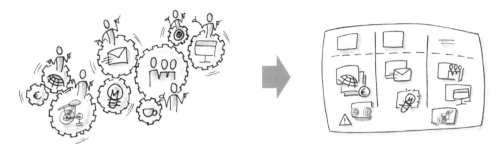

HOW THE SYSTEM WORKS   HOW WE VISUALISE IT

Figure 3.7 – Visualizing your system is a skill

What actually ends up on the wall is a reflection of the thought process of the team and their understanding of the system. You can read a lot from just walking into an Obeya about the team and where they are in their process. It reflects what they think is important, how they go about organizing themselves, how they see their performance and what they are improving.

WHERE VISUAL MANAGEMENT COMES FROM

Examples of the use of visual management go back a long time. A well-known system for visual management applied to professional work environments is Kanban. The first application of Kanban (translates to "sign board" or "visual card" in Japanese), a system that uses cards and aims to ensure a system provides "(1) what is needed, (2) at the time needed, (3) in the amount needed" (Ohno, 1978) dates back to 1953 at Toyota. By studying American supermarkets, Toyota developed a system that works on a pull principle: to deliver according to customer need. Through this elegant system, they reduced planning efforts, cost of carrying inventory, overproduction, waiting times, etc.

BENEFITS OF VISUAL MANAGEMENT

The intention of visualizing your work process is not for the sake of visualization. It requires hard work and focused concentration by the team, but that enables joint learning and improving activities. And that's where the value is — working on your system, together, acknowledging each other's experience and skills and expertise to create a visual common frame of reference.

Visualization itself is never a solution to anything, the value is in the efforts of the team during the visualization process and the meetings that follow thereafter: to baseline their work, identify problems and solve them to get better at what they do.

In addition to uncovering new information about the system that you work in, visual management can also help build contextual continuity. Humans are naturally limited in the amount and complexity of information that we can process. Having the visual context present whenever we make decisions will help us shift our attention to the right things, and make decisions with all relevant information at hand.[41]

If you're in a leadership position you'll be expected to make important decisions on a regular basis. But did you know your memory decay starts after as little as thirty seconds (Todd & Marois, 2004)?[42] Using visual management helps increase engagement, helps us focus on what's important, helps our memory with readily available facts and provides a meaningful context for reflection and debate to make the right decisions.

> **TIP** - Don't depend on visuals to give you all the answers. The visuals are in fact there to help you ask the right questions. If you have a question that cannot be answered with the visuals, then you might be exploring a part of the system you haven't visualized yet. The next question would be: (1) Is this a relevant question and (2) Should we spend time structurally exposing the answers to this question?

A COUPLE OF POINTERS

Pierre Masai, CIO of Toyota Europe, explains his experience with visual management at Toyota (2017).[43] "Whenever you walk into a Toyota office (be it in HR, logistics or purchasing) one is able to quickly grasp what is happening by looking at the visualizations on the office walls." This should be the goal of visual management: see, learn and act. Which design guidelines can we apply that help with quickly grasping the situation in your Obeya?

1. Look at the whole picture

Following the principle of thinking in systems, we try to visualize the whole system in the Obeya, at the level of detail which is relevant for the team. We do this by visualizing the five key responsibilities for leadership as discussed in Part V, which together encompass everything that concerns the act of leading the organization.

Figure 3.8 – Five areas to represent the whole picture

2. Help focus on what's important

Agreeing on the "standard mode of operations," — identifying thresholds for performance (for example, we expect to produce 80 bikes a week) — helps identify exceptions and problems. As such, you'll be able to ask valuable questions such as: What *did not* go according to what was expected? What caused the deviation? What was the root cause? What can we learn? Those are the core questions to be asked when looking at deviations from the plan, because they often point us to valuable improvements in our system.

Figure 3.9 – Using red/green signaling to guide focus during meetings

3. Flow of information and simple, accessible visual structures

Make it easy to find the right information (the structure helps you find the relevant information instead of having to sift through thirty report pages). By presenting complex information in such a way, the team can easily follow the logic, perhaps guided by visual icons, markers, lines, etc. This requires the room be structured in a logical way, information flows logically through lanes, there is no overlap of information, etc.

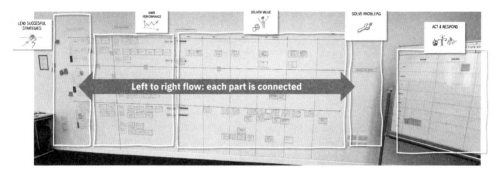

Figure 3.10 – Left to right flow example

4. Neat looking visuals engaging both sides of the brain

No matter how you go about it, always try to stimulate both aspects of the brain: logic and creativity. Logic is in the numbers and breakdown of contextual information, supporting the scientific thinking. Creativity is in the use of colors, drawings, iconizing, using pictures for the team members or even avatars. The latter will help make things stick to memory by addressing multiple areas of the brain. This will also help create a stronger sense of ownership in the room as well as identification with the metrics and goals. A vivid image is one which you have a high likelihood of retrieving its sensory details. Visuals help focus attention and enhance short term "working memory." If things are on top of mind we are more likely to engage with them.

TIP - If you don't like what you're seeing, look again. It is important to understand that your ability to visualize how your system works will contribute to the actual working of the system. However, if you do not visualize it well, it does not necessarily mean your system is broken, it can also mean you simply need to improve your understanding and visualization of that system. Moreover, every step towards visualization is likely to expose problems. Hence, if the visualization doesn't seem to work for you, take a step back and observe what's really going on – you might have exposed a problem that you can now start to solve.

Develop people

Developing people is a directly related to respect for people, which is one of the pillars of the Toyota Production System. If you wonder how, then let's look at the following train of thought:

- If you hire someone and you give them targets for their work, but do not spend serious time developing their capabilities in the context of your organization, is it fair to expect them to meet every target they're given?
- If a person goes off, figuring out the best way to achieve an objective, is it respectful to have them figure out the best way of doing it, while someone else already knows the best known way? Would it be beneficial for the organization to let them find out for themselves or with minimum amounts of instruction?

Starting with Obeya means you're on a path of continuous learning, but also continuous teaching of what was learned. In the Obeya, the skills to develop on a leadership level are inherently related to the Reference Model: the visuals on the wall, and the principles for learning and acting.

For example, the principle of "Share context & problems visually" is an important step in learning and development for a leadership team, and is practiced when they start visualizing their system while setting up their Obeya for the first time.

CONSISTENCY IN LEADERSHIP

The visualization process exposes how each member of the leadership team (likely) has a different view on how their leadership and value systems work. It will also expose points for development or learning by looking at the way people in the team think and act. This is useful for any team at any given moment. Why? The different views not only expose different levels of knowledge and expertise, but may also lead to inconsistencies in processes and application of policies towards operational teams. That causes variation in policy execution, which in turn leads to potentially bigger inconsistencies for customers, which leads to problems, waste, etc.

The leadership responsibility areas in the Obeya each represent a leadership skill that can and should be developed. Take "Deliver Value" for example, where a leader must take portfolio decisions: which products will we develop first, given our limited resources? If one department makes these choices in a very different way than the other, then you might have an alignment problem if these two departments are both needed to deliver end-to-end value to the customer.

It's safe to say that the five leadership responsibility areas can be captured in a way of working that can be rolled out over an organization, and that this will bring great benefits in terms of alignment, cohesion and consistency, because on a systems level we're all using the same way of working. That seems to make sense, right?

Imagine if we turned it around, if we said "hey, you go and figure out how you want to prioritize your projects and I'll just do it my way." What would that do to the consistency and alignment in our organization? It doesn't make sense to do it this way, right? But it might be exactly what your organization is doing today.

What happens when somebody who will be acting in a leadership position joins your company.? How would that person be helped to understand the strategy and their contributions to it? Do you have an onboarding process which covers that? Great, but how is that person's development supported thereafter? Will their behavior and ways of doing things rely mostly on what they're used to doing? Let's assume new blood is good, new ideas, creative thoughts, etc. That is a valuable thing, indeed.

But how will we ensure we stay aligned with what that individual and their teams are doing? How do we make sure the new team member adopts all the valuable lessons and ways of working that we have carefully developed within our organization?

LEADERSHIP RESPONSIBILITY FOR DEVELOPING PEOPLE IN OPERATIONAL TEAMS

Taking responsibility for the development of people is crucial to develop the necessary capabilities in the organization, and, as such, be able to achieve the purpose. Not just development of leadership, but especially development of people that spend most of their time in work that actually adds value to customers.

Developing people can hardly be "outsourced" to people managers, external trainers or coaches. The people in operational teams perform activities that are the core task of the company. It is in fact the task of the manager or leader to facilitate the development of the people in his or her team in such a way that value is delivered to customers in an even better way, and the organization's purpose is actively pursued. The task for facilitating people and teams on an operational level should be focused on letting them thrive on a personal and professional level, as well as making that person and the team they operate in capable of contributing to the overall strategy. Let's not forget, the real value is delivered by operational teams.

Sharing information on how to do things is great, but is no guarantee that people will act accordingly. Sending a person on a training is nice and will inspire them, but once they get back to their normal workplace where nothing has changed they won't put much of it in practice. So what else must we do to develop people?

THREE ASPECTS OF PEOPLE DEVELOPMENT IN THE OBEYA

Essentially developing people in the Obeya is threefold:

1. The leadership team members are developed through practice in the responsibility areas and application of the principles: a coach helps them see what they overlook and adopt effective habits.
2. Members of your leadership team learn to become coaches through practicing coaching Kata with individuals from their teams, working on challenges that have a direct relationship with key success factors we identified in the Obeya. Leaders learn to be coaches as a skill.

3. Individuals from your operational teams are involved in the Obeya and are being taught to follow the improvement Kata through coaching by their team leader. They're learning improvement thinking patterns, skills and behaviors.

COACHING KATA

Wax on, wax off. We learn best by being engaged with what we learn and through practice. Leaders are required to actually spend time with people in their teams. And leaders need to learn the skill of people development. A good way to do this is for leaders to apply the Coaching Kata (Rother, 2009)[44], which is a routine that can be learned and practiced with help of another coach.

The idea is simple: there are five questions which a leader on any level of the organization will ask to whomever he or she will be having an "improvement" session with. Usually, this is done at the Solve Problems area, to make sure that what is being worked on is linked to key aspects in the Obeya.

The five questions are as follows[*]:
1. What is the target condition?
2. What is the actual condition now?
3. Which obstacles do you think are preventing you from reaching the target condition? Which one are you addressing now?
4. What is the next step (experiment)? What do you expect?
5. How quickly can we see what we have learned from that step?

Asking these questions and practicing the coaching Kata looks deceitfully easy, but it is not. Ask the questions in a slightly different way and you might get a completely different answer, or even change the relationship with the person you're doing the Kata with. For example, not asking for what was learned, but asking for the result might trigger a person to think that you're after results, not learnings. And in a Management by Objectives environment, you're right back to people aiming and gaming for results, rather than improving their skills to improve the system that delivers those results.

[*]   Please refer to Mike Rother's free materials on Toyota Kata at: http://www-personal.umich.edu/~mrother/The_Coaching_Kata.html

In any case, the coaching Kata helps but it should be appropriately used, and anybody who starts with it should respect the fact that it takes a long time to master. Remember, we have a tendency to overestimate ourselves. As Malcolm Gladwell, author of *Outliers*, who came up with the 10,000 hour rule for skill acquisition explains, "The amount of time necessary to develop your abilities is probably longer than you think"[45]. Also, developing the skill to develop people will take a bit of time to truly master.

Development of people isn't something you start and then stop once they reach a maturity level. It's a continuous activity which is given more or less priority based on what capabilities must be developed to achieve the purpose of your organization.

By connecting mentors and improvers from all levels of the organization, a coherent structure appears of bottom-up learning and top-down strategic governance with a feedback loop that is unprecedented in traditional ways of management.

Concluding the review of this principle, we can say the Obeya is a platform for learning and teaching. In fact, a few principles from *The Toyota Way*[46] related to learning and teaching should be literally practiced by leadership in the Obeya:"

- Grow leaders who thoroughly understand the work, live the philosophy, and teach it to others.
- Develop exceptional people and teams who follow your company's philosophy.
- Become a learning organization through relentless reflection and continuous improvement.

Figure 3.11 – Increase the effect of learning and improving through coaching on each level

Rhythm & Routine (Kata)

WHAT IS DISCUSSED DURING MEETINGS IN THE OBEYA?

The short answer is: anything that contributes to achieving your strategic goals and requires you to make decisions or act based on shared context. If we zoom in a little, we find there are recurring meetings for each of the Visual Areas in the Reference Model. Let's take one of the examples from Part I and see what is discussed in each area to get a taste of it. These areas have a rhythm and routine specifically designed to develop consistently executed leadership skills for each area. You will find more specifics for each meeting in Part IV.

Figure 3.12 – Each area has its own rhythm and routine

Lead Successful Strategies

In this area, the team agrees on the purpose and strategic capabilities needed to fulfill that purpose. This is derived from the overall strategy of the organization.

Drive Performance

Here the team works on uncovering the performance of their organization both internally (e.g. employee satisfaction) and externally (e.g. customer satisfaction). By setting targets, the team knows where they stand today, where they want to be and how to prioritize improvements to get there.

Solve Problems

If the team finds they are trying to stabilize or improve performance but the solution to making that happen is obscured, they will begin structured problem solving: uncovering new parts of the system and setting challenges that help them up their game.

Deliver Value

The team prioritizes the work in a portfolio discussion, assigns capacity to the prioritized work and aligns on the roadmap towards future development of their value adding activities such as building new features for their website. This meeting is often aligned with planning meetings of operational teams that do sprints.

Act & Respond

Brief, short meetings that help understand what's going on quickly, acting and responding to new developments. Also, a very important meeting must be available to align and address problems or requests raised by teams from work floor or upper management.

*"I think the way of working with Obeya as we implement-
ed it now works really well. It provides a place to gather
with a fixed agenda to focus on results. Before this I really missed the flow of information, I had to personally go
and fetch the information I needed from a Product Owner or a Scrum Master, finding out what was going on in
the teams. If you have about twenty squads and around
170 people in a tribe, it's a mission impossible to keep
track on what was going on. The traditional meeting
structure was much more individual, incidental and ad
hoc, there was very little structure. However in the Obeya
meeting you just witnessed you could see by looking at
our "energy meter" how the energy levels of the participants have risen during the meeting."*

– Sytze Hiemstra, Tribe Lead

THE MESSY SCHEDULE OF A MANAGER

Is your daily work schedule as messy as most managers? Do you try to squeeze in
more meetings in an already full schedule, run a bit later on every next meeting, and
have the feeling you're actually not getting any value out of it?

Usually, if you're in a leadership position, your agenda is a challenge by itself. The
first problem is that meetings are everywhere and you're schedule's simply fully
booked. The second challenge is that you leave a lot of these meetings and feel in
your gut that it has to be possible to get a lot more results out of them. Sometimes,
discussions get so lengthy we're not even able to get through all the topics on the
agenda, which means you'll have to wait another two weeks before getting a decision on your proposal.

No rhythm: high variability lots of planning effort

Rhythm: predictable, efficient, fast

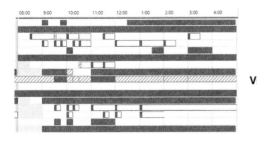

Vs.

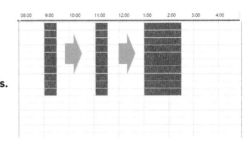

Figure 3.13 – A rhythm helps the team be available to requests by other teams and avoids unnecessary planning efforts to setup meetings

On many occasions I have met leaders that were either late or cancelled meetings completely at the last minute simply because other meetings were more important, they were running late or their priority apparently wasn't on their meeting with me. Also, many of the managers I met accepted this issue, coming late to almost every meeting, keeping members of their team waiting and seemingly running behind on things that needed to be discussed. It seems like this is just the fate of the manager and nothing can be done about it.

But what if we could do something about it? What if meetings don't have to run late, what if they follow a predictable flow and pace and align in such a way that one meeting prepares you for the other?

See if you can get more structure and free up time by adopting a rhythm, allowing a few key meetings to take care of most of your responsibilities as a leader. If all goes well, a manager should be able to fulfill most if their responsibilities for their team in about eight hours per week. That only works if you are willing to cancel existing meetings that will overlap with the purpose of the Obeya meetings. If you do, you'll be able to get into a pretty effective meeting structure. For example:

Less than eight hours per week to fully align with your leadership team

1x 1.5 hour Drive Performance or Deliver Value	=	1.5 hour
3x 0.5 hour Act & Respond	=	1.5 hour
4x (2x 30 minutes) Solve Problems	=	4 hours
0.5x 1.5 hour content / deep dive meetings	=	45 minutes
Total	**=**	**7 hours and 45 minutes**

In practice, you could take care of almost all your leadership responsibilities within your leadership team in just one day's effort. That includes spending time with members of your teams to work on structured problem solving, which is usually the first topic to be disregarded when the going gets tough.

Don't be mistaken, if you look at your agenda right now and try to add another eight hours of meetings your mind will disconnect with any opportunity to start with Obeya meetings. However, if you clear your mind and start thinking about what should be essential meetings that are critical to executing your task, without the irrational demand for seemingly pointless meetings of your organization currently, these Obeya meetings will make a lot of sense. So try to be mindful about your current schedule and see which session can be replaced, realigned or even removed from your agenda to free up time so you can perform your tasks properly.

> *"It's not just about what's being added, but more importantly what will be removed from your agenda. There were a few specific examples like a monthly meeting where we used to discuss how things are going. Now we do this more frequently in less time. It brings us more quality in the meeting, but also we're able to respond to developments much faster than before."*
>
> **– Sytze Hiemstra, Tribe Lead**

A DIFFERENT WAY TO LOOK AT MEETINGS

All of the Obeya meeting routines work together as one, addressing all aspects of management: setting direction, planning change, running operations, doing improvements, following up actions.

The areas and, therefore, the meetings are interlinked, with improvement being the central theme and driver for all others. Because they are all linked, if you miss out on one, it will impact performance of the others.

For example, having a performance and a portfolio area without the context of a strategy area will make it difficult to determine guidance towards principal discussions of priority, direction or even alignment for the team. Likewise, if there was a portfolio wall but no action board, then there would be no fast follow-up of actions and decisions, severely slowing down the responsiveness of the team and potentially delaying results as priorities are only monitored once every two weeks.

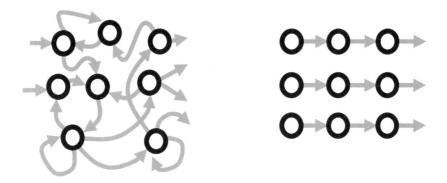

Figure 3.14 – From chaotic meetings to structured routines

Adopting a fixed rhythm is also very practical in terms of predictability. Once you know you're meeting three times a week on Tuesday, Wednesday and Thursday, you can anticipate it and so can others. Many teams today are already adopting a rhythm in their schedules, like the daily stand-up used in Scrum and the planning and retrospective sessions in a fixed time window during the sprint.

If there is no habit, we'll be asking ourselves regularly "when is that meeting again?" We'll also check our schedules at least once a week and look up the new meeting time and date to anticipate that meeting. Now imagine we had that same meeting every Monday at 10:00 am.

Then imagine, at some point, we'd be so good at having that meeting every Monday we would be able to finish all our work in it and have time left for the things we never got around to.

Imagine if we could start using a meeting rhythm not just for ourselves, but also with other teams. In this way we can make sure that whenever we discuss something in one meeting, any outcome could immediately be taken into the next.

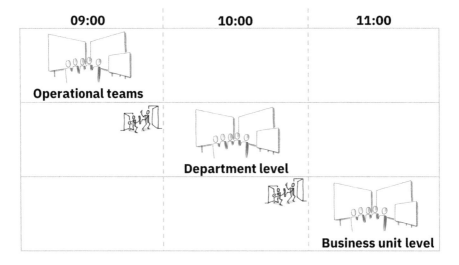

Figure 3.15 – Passing the baton after each meeting, enabling a cascade

People are creatures of habit, and doing things routinely creates new, desirable habits that offer a way to promote mental fitness towards the task of leadership through structure and organization.

In the Obeya, each Kata is connected to the other. This way, information finds its way fast and effectively into the next point for decision-making. As such, problems do not have to wait weeks for the next management meeting to get approval because the meeting took place yesterday.

ROUTINE: MASTERING THE LEADERSHIP MOVES

In order to truly exercise all of the key leadership activities with your leadership team, you'll need to become really effective when you do have meetings. Conducting these meetings is a skill. It can and must be learned in order to achieve the benefits.

The word "Kata", when translated from martial arts like Karate, Aikido and Jiujit-su, means form or shape. It is a centuries old way of transferring capabilities from one person to another. In karate, it is used to practice individual moves that when combined and appropriately timed form the shape and technique used in a man to man fight. Each shape is specifically designed in relation to its purpose and puts its related principles into practice.

There is a reason this principle is at the entry door of the Obeya Reference Model. The application of principles into practice is essentially what we're trying to do with the application of Kata through a rhythm and routine in the Obeya. Each individual move (meeting) makes up the total moves needed in the actual fight.

With practice on a routine basis, a person creates more neural pathways, strengthening their capability to perform the routine effectively, hence getting more out of their meetings. Adding rhythm to your moves will help you develop a capability to take on every challenge at the right time, and with enough practice be on the way to your organization's path to glory.

In martial arts, the opponent is standing right in front of you, but in the Obeya, your challengers are the problems and challenges you face as a leadership team. You need to learn to do this with the right timing and with the ability to deliver the right punch on the right spot. The more you practice, the more skilled you will become at achieving your purpose.

Tuning your rhythm and routine will help you tackle problems faster and more effectively so as not to slow down your teams and maximize delivery of value.

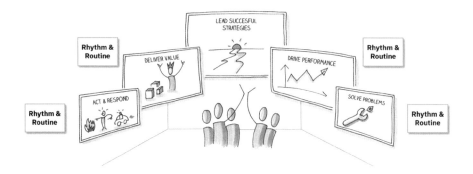

Figure 3.16 – Place the routines physically near the related area

The routine in the Obeya is located at each area and used in every session. Doing the facilitation strictly to the routine helps the team be mindful of what's happening in the organization at the right moment and the right time. Instead of taking whatever pops up in our mind first (for example the email you read last evening, or the conversation you had this morning).

Moreover, routines help activate System 2 thinking by providing enough time and practice so that the effort of doing the meeting itself is reduced and more System 2 processing power can go to making effective decisions.

Asking the right questions

> *"Sometimes I compare the routine with a SIM card: you cannot place it incorrectly. The routine does the same, it helps you ask exactly those questions that matter."*
>
> **– Liedewij van der Scheer, Lean Black Belt**

The quality of discussions is also improved by avoiding bias through the use of question formulation that avoids noise in the answers that we get. The way a question is worded greatly determines the answer that you'll get (Kahneman, 2009)[47].

Both formulation of the right questions and proper facilitation by a coach or facilitator are needed to avoid bias and make better decisions.

Examples of ambiguous or biased questions:
- *How can we solve this problem as soon as possible?* You may remove symptoms and reduce impact of a problem quickly, but this question doesn't entice people to take time to get to the root cause and implement a sustainable solution to prevent the problem from occurring again.
- *This team has a lower velocity than the other Scrum teams. How can we increase velocity of this Scrum team?* Velocity is not a comparable measurement of productivity.
- *We must make better margins, how can we reduce costs?* You're troubleshooting without understanding the problem, reducing costs isn't the only way to improve margins.
- *This meeting is taking too long, can we schedule less time next time?* If the meeting is taking too long, you're either doing it ineffectively or you simply need the time because of an agenda with too many topics. So spending less time is not going to solve a problem.

Use routines to create new habits

Neurons are firing in our brain each time we are thinking or doing something. The more they are fired in the same direction, the stronger the pathway, or synapses, become. Hence, if we do something often, we will grow a strong neural pathway.

Now comes the trick. Stronger neural pathways make it easier to go down that road again. It won't cost us a lot of effort and sometimes we even do it almost unconsciously. When the going gets tough, this is what we'll resort to. Based on the situation we're in, we'll activate these pathways. For example when our shoelaces are untied, we'll come to the quick solution to tie them. When we are tying we don't think of the exact movements anymore, we just do them. That's a simple solution to a simple problem.

But the challenge arises when we are confronted with a need or desire to change something we've always been used to doing. This is sometimes needed. When we change our strategy it may also imply we want to change the way we work. If that new way of working is new to us, we'll need to learn new neural pathways and it'll take a while before they are as strong and efficient as the old ones. In fact, you cannot unlearn neural pathways so they are always lurking about, driving you and people around you back to old behavior that may be contradicting in terms of the new strategy we've just decided on. Scientists studying addiction believe that the old habits cannot be unlearned, they must be replaced by something new. That's why quitting smoking is so hard if you cannot replace the urge to go down the neural highway of smoking a cigarette with something else.

If we want to focus our minds effectively on the new strategy or way of working, then we'll have to find a way to create new and strong neural pathways. In the Obeya this is why we introduce a regular rhythm and a routine. That means we have regular intervals of practicing a certain way of thinking and behavior on the job to create those new pathways. By aligning those pathways with the application of principles and use of the visuals in the Obeya, the team becomes more and more effective with each session.

Figure 3.17 – Meeting in the Obeya

RHYTHM: FAST RESPONSE TO CHANGE AND PROBLEMS

The routines are the meetings that help you address the challenges, and the rhythm determines how often you practice your skills in the meeting and take on problems (invisible opponents) as they come along.

"The overall rhythm of your Kata depends entirely on how fast you choose to dispose of these invisible opponents."

– Jesse Enkamp, Karate Nerd

For this reason, each routine has its own rhythm that caters to the type of problem the team needs to address. Are they in need of quick responses because they suddenly appear and are blocking teams from delivering value? The Act & Respond rhythm will be able pick up any problem as it arises from the stand-up of an operational team in the morning because the leadership team gathers at least three times a week. However, problems that are more on a level of strategic policy, for example, whether customers are responding to the new marketing campaign, or whether they are still happily using our products one month after their purchase, are typically problems that take a bit longer to uncover. That's why we address those once every two weeks in the Deliver Value and Drive Performance meetings.

Applying the principle of having fixed rhythms and routines for your meeting is beneficial in many ways. To name a few:

- Being available to your teams regularly (instead of them having trouble to get in touch with you because your schedule is all over the place).
- Being available fast, avoiding the postponement of problems because we have to wait until the next bi-weekly management meeting before they can be scheduled on the overcrowded agenda.
- Ensuring you have enough time during your scheduled meetings to actually tackle those problems that matter most, rather than leaving every meeting feeling you didn't get enough done.

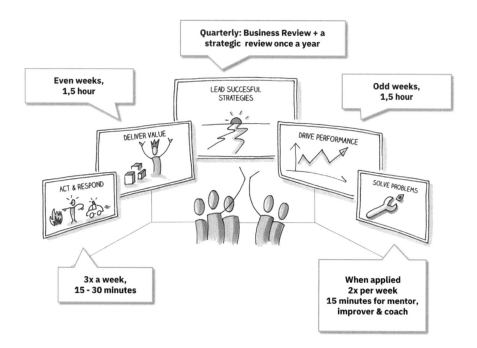

Figure 3.18 – Overview of Obeya with rhythm

Some teams do have a rhythm for their meetings, but it either doesn't allot for enough time, doesn't occur many enough times a week or they don't have a suitable routine that helps them address all items on the agenda. They might run out of time because not enough time has been reserved, or they try to squeeze in more topics than time permits for the next meeting. Essentially, they're pushing (not pulling) topics for discussion into the next meeting.

If that's the case, there is a risk important things might fall off the agenda and teams may not be supported, for example, with resolving problems. If it's then another week or so before the next attempt to address the problem, your team will be impeded from delivering maximum value during this time unless they can force decisions outside of the existing meeting structure through escalation.

Escalations, when done outside of a meeting structure that caters for fast routing of problems to the right level of decision making, are (or should be) exceptional events because they distract leaders from doing their normal work. If you have a lot of them because the normal meeting and decision making structure is not suitable to address problems at the right level in a fast and effective way, then your leadership is bound to be distracted with escalations from bottom-up and top-down, dragging them into fire-fighting mode and preventing them from making long-term sustainable improvements.

How this will help you spend your time more effectively

Working with a rhythm and routine will not make your need to have meetings go away, but they will definitely help you spend your time more effectively.

It doesn't seem like much, but try opening your schedule for last week and seeing how many ad hoc meetings you had that required your brain computing time to figure out where to go at what time and how to prepare for that meeting? How much time did you spend in the evenings trying to prepare for meetings, sharing context with others that need updates from you?

Here are a few examples of how you benefit from having the right rhythm & routine with your teams:

1. You won't have to spend time scheduling meetings in everybody's agenda and sorting out meeting rooms (which is effectively non-value add time).
2. The predictability of a rhythm means people that commit to this timeframe are more likely to prevent double booking of meetings, requiring rescheduling or spending more time on the phone to find a free spot in your agenda's.
3. It helps create and adopt a pattern that requires less brain capacity. Remember our System 2 access is limited. When a meeting is shifting every week it will literally require more computing time in our brains to work out when to go where. That time would be better spent in the actual meeting.
4. By involving the right people in the meetings and optimizing the rhythm so that information travels fast within the organization, managers need less time on ad hoc updates to ensure people are informed and aligned. This is likely a large portion of time consumption for a traditional manager.
5. When we are required to think and act on many various unrelated topics during the day, our brains require 'changeover time'. We need to reset our working memory to adjust for the new topic that requires our attention.

This happens when we have many different, short interactions via email, phone, various unrelated meetings, etc. But when we are able to redirect many of these brain-capacity demanding impulses and bundle them to the right meetings, we can combine relevant topics in the same meeting, requiring less changeover time, increasing the availability of our System 2 thinking.

6. Making decisions is a key task for managers. But you need to have the right information to make the right decision. What if you can avoid ad hoc requests coming at you in all sorts of shapes and sizes? What if the next time a project manager comes up to you with the request to make a decision, he or she has a short but structured problem statement, motivation and request, providing all relevant information for you in a context where all information that you need to make that decision is available on the walls in big room? How much time would you be able to save if all your project managers learned how to do that and did it in the same way in the same meeting?

7. Out of all the ad hoc requests coming at you as a manager on a daily basis, how do you prioritize which ones to pick up in the limited time available to you? How can you set a priority on project A, if your colleague in the leadership time might decide to make a priority out of project B that day? By converging requests through the Obeya sessions, you can make a team decision on which requests to prioritize so you can rest assured they are aligned, which will greatly increase the effect of your work.

TIP - For each problem or challenge that is addressed in your meetings, try and establish whether you're happy with (1) the time it took between recognizing the problem at its source, (2) the quality with which the problem and related question was addressed to your team (e.g. did you understand it, was the impact clear so you could prioritize?), and (3) how fast you can get it to the right person to start studying and solving it.

"Having Obeya meetings gives the leadership team a lot more energy. They may start skeptical and surprised at first, but pretty soon they discover it is radically different and interesting for them. Before they were having a meeting with a full agenda and a lot of time pressure. The right conversation doesn't take place there. Instead they find the Obeya meetings more effective."

– Jeroen Venneman, Agile Coach & Transformation Consultant

Go & See

LIMITATIONS OF REPORTS

As we've learned in Part II, we are biased and prone to making assumptions. The size and complexity of some organizations make it hard for management to maintain a daily presence, or any presence at all on the work floor. They become disconnected from the Production System; they don't really know how things work in the operational teams.

A gap exists between work floor teams and "them" — the management. However, they are still expected to make sensible decisions about the Production System, and to do so they need some form of information that will provide them with information to substantiate and validate their decisions. Hence, the reporting structure is born.

Though the principle of abstracting information from the work floor isn't necessarily a bad one by itself, in practice it does lead to undesirable effects and pitfalls, to name a few:

- **The waste of administrative overburden** – teams spend too much time on daily or weekly reports that are, in fact, not used, or sparsely used.

- **Abstraction** – details are lost when the actual situation on the work floor is summarized in a Red Amber Green (RAG) status and a few bullets, and the details that are included in the report depend highly on the capability of its author.
- **Answering the wrong or an ambiguous question** – If a manager asks his team, "How is it going here?" they might respond in a variety of ways, like: "Good, a six out of ten," or, "We are three days behind schedule but we're confident we can catch up." In the report this is likely to show up as "green," but what does that really mean and how can a manager act on this?
- **Political interest by the reporter** - Its author, or worse, his or her senior manager, may have an agenda of interest that conflicts, for example, with the objec tive exposure of a problem in case it prevents a KPI to be met or could lead to signs of incapability.
- **Several forms of bias or fallacies for readers / senior managers** – These lurk around when senior managers read reports and use the limited and subjective information or their frame of mind to make decisions for whether or not to act upon the information. Remember your brain's limitations for failing in strategic execution?

LOOKING AT INFORMATION IN THE OBEYA

Given the fact the Obeya is full of reports, we should spend some time on how to avoid the pitfalls just mentioned. The key is to go see, and be involved in the process where the information originates as well as the process of how the report is created.

Since the role of the manager is to facilitate the operational operations to ensure maximum creation of value, it is also the responsibility of the manager to make sure the right information for quality decision making is provided to enable the development of capabilities of and by teams.

So how can a manager assume his or her role in creating quality reports?
1. Using improvement Kata / scientific method to create reports.
2. Leadership involvement and accountability in making reports.
3. Assume the information for basis of discussion in the Obeya is on the wall, not in emails, letters, hearsay, etc.
4. Avoid bias and do not fill in the gaps. Go & See where the data comes from:

   the work floor.

GOING TO THE WORK FLOOR

Empiricism is an important part of working with Lean & Agile. Empiricism suggests we learn from practice, and practice in terms of work and realizing strategy happens almost entirely in one place: the work floor. Strengthening the connection with operational teams and their activities on the work floor is a valuable thing to do for any leader who wishes to achieve effective operations towards achievement of their purpose. After all, it's the activities on the work floor that sum up the value that is being achieved for customers, strategic goals and purpose of the organization.

So how can we truly, honestly gather useful data for decision-making with the goal to facilitate teams through objectives, goals and purpose? Simply by avoiding pitfalls caused by abstraction or interpretation: go to the source of the data.

Usually this is where the work actually happens, also referred to as "Gemba" in Lean context. To many, going to the source of the data, spending time to investigate, gathering facts and context from people close to it to make a better decision will sound like common sense. In Lean, "collecting facts and data at the actual site of the work or problem" is referred to as "Genchi Gembutsu" (Sutherland & Bennett, 2007)[48].

Leaders should Go & See where the work happens to gather facts. In knowledge worker environments it is hard or impossible to see the work unless the work floor or other teams have in fact started to use visual management.

In each central area of work, be it a team, a monitoring function, a product area or a Leadership Obeya, the work should be visualized. There should be a standard of that work to explain to the rest of the organization's members how work is done, what the standard thresholds for performance are and which problems are being solved. Only then will a leader be able to Go & See and get the facts in a meaningful way.

RESPECT FOR PEOPLE

People closest to the problem typically know the most about it. If you want people in your organization that are both effective and motivated, leaders must learn to both lead and be respectful of people and their work efforts.

Simply walking down the hallway, looking over the shoulders of one of your team members and asking them performance related questions is probably going to create some anxious moments. Visits by leaders to the work floor (or Gemba in Lean context), are sometimes referred to as Gallery Walks. The reason being that so much is preorganized and announced around the visit of the leader that much of what he or she will find on the work floor is artificial rather than a representation of the real work floor (e.g. cleaning has been done, metrics updated, Kanban boards updated). This is not a great setting for an honest dialogue in which learning and mentoring can take place.

Keep improving

THE SAGA OF CONTINUOUS IMPROVEMENT

The promise of systemic, continuous improvement for organizations has been around since scientific thinking hit the world of management, say around the start of the 1900's when Frederick Winslow Taylor (1911) introduced scientific thinking to organizations in the industrial age.[49] It does make sense to a lot of people to test if your improvement activities have, in fact, resulted in increased performance for your organization, and to systematically keep improving for better outcomes.

Other important influencers in the 20th Century, building on continuous improvement, were Shewhart and Deming[*] who were involved in boosting the Japanese auto industry in the 1950s. The Shewhart cycle's latest version was published by Deming in 1993 as the PDSA cycle.[50] As you can see this cycle of continuous improvement essentially summarizes many of the practices seen today that originate from Lean or Agile ways of working.

---

[*] Note that some will refer to PDCA as the 'Deming cycle', which is fake news according to Deming in two ways: 1. It is was originally the Shewhart cycle, named after Demings mentor who came up with it, and 2. Deming disapproves of the modifications made to Shewhart's cycle as the Check suggests you stop and do a quick check if the results are as expected, while the Study in his 1993 model implies the pursuit of actual learnings through study.

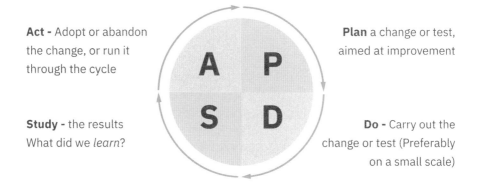

Figure 3.19 – PDSA cycle from Deming's 1993 book The New Economics

So there's been quite a history of continuous improvement dating back to early last century. There seems to be something in our brains that logically agrees with continuous improvement, but lacks the ability to put it into practice. Why is that?

Management by Objectives doesn't allow time for learning

You can only improve continuously if you learn. But learning often isn't part of a culture that was raised and taught to meet objectives. Management by Objectives suggests you achieve targets, and in the achievement of targets, learning slows you down as the act of learning is not immediately tied to a measurable business outcome target. In fact, one could argue that in a Management By Objectives perspective, learning is a waste, and it is treated as such, because the instant the going gets tough, we resort to firefighting and troubleshooting. Now don't get me wrong, when the house is on fire you should use all your System 1 thinking capacity to either fight the fire effectively or get yourself to safety. But if this is the only mode we tend to use, then we'll never be able to improve our homes and fires will keep coming.

We're used to not wanting to see problems since in an MBO environment problems show we're on a path of failure. But from the principle of improvement, not revealing problems means you're not able to improve simply because you cannot see where you must improve. It's like running blindfolded towards a target with obvious results.

Remember the guy that's trying to chop down the tree with an axe, too busy to talk to the guy next to him offering a chainsaw? Some claim they don't have time to work on improvements because they are too busy doing their work.

Something that seems like a good idea is easily forgotten the moment your go back to doing what you've always done. Chakravorty (2010)[51] compares attempts at continuous improvement with the attempt to lose weight and suggests these attempts "fail to have a lasting impact as participants gradually lose motivation and fall back into old habits." Their research shows almost 60% of the continuous improvement initiatives did not succeed due to the lack of habit creation. So even though everybody will agree the PDSA cycle makes a lot of sense, we fail to put it in practice if we cannot find ways to make continuous improvement a habitual exercise.

MOVING FROM ACHIEVING TO LEARNING

Learning is the central theme in the Obeya, meaning that Management By Objectives (e.g. through typical RAG reporting) is replaced by continuous improvement of people and processes. The latter meaning that management doesn't focus on outcome, but rather the process that creates that outcome.

Research indicates this is not only a more effective approach, but also a healthier one. Carol Dweck (2012) refers to the difference as a growth mindset and a fixed mindset. The fixed mindset says that achievement of a goal whether you either fail or succeed. If you do fail, you're a loser. If you win, you're smart. But the problem is, this doesn't foster self-esteem or lead to accomplishment, but may actually jeopardize success because it doesn't invoke learning.

The growth mindset is all about learning. It does not matter how intelligent you are, it's about learning and learning helps you make better, more knowledgeable decisions. So instead of rewarding the outcome, the effort of learning is appreciated and encouraged. Dweck's research shows kids to be happier and better performers when they grow up in an environment where a growth mindset is stimulated. This is exactly the kind of thinking we're looking for in the Obeya.

"If our business philosophy and management approach do not include constant adaptiveness and improvement, then companies and their leaders can get stuck in patterns that grow less and less applicable in changing circumstances"

– Mike Rother, Toyota Kata

Adopting a continuous improvement way of thinking and acting affects how problems are being identified, addressed, how much trust is given and accountability is taken. To some managers who have ingrained a traditional management style during all of their career, it will require a significant paradigm shift; suddenly a red flag is good, because we exposed a problem, rather than it meaning disappointment, anger or even punishment is on the way. To introduce this way of thinking and acting really means changing underlying beliefs and habits that you are likely to have been raised with all your life. Having a coach guide you in this process as an external conscience should be a very serious consideration. On top of that, following an improvement pattern that will help you with asking the right questions that promote the growth mindset also helps.

TIP - The Obeya itself is a tool, and as such it is something you and your team must learn to master. Here are a few practical suggestions to help you improve your ability to use Obeya:
- Close every routine with a reflective question for learning and improvement
- Organize periodic retrospectives
- Use a Tcian system, in which users can drop improvements in an improvement inbox which can then be discussed during the retrospective.
- Use the Leading With Obeya – Reference Model and descriptions in this book as a reference to determine if all elements are there and doing what they should do. Use it as a coaching model to refer to problems that are experienced during sessions and where they might be in the model.

Solving problems that are holding us back

Starting your Obeya endeavor with the agreement on the definition of a Problem* is a very useful, practical thing to do. It would be wrong to assume we all look at problems the same way. What might be a problem to you might be completely irrelevant for me. It depends on our understanding or problems, in what way it affects us and how deeply we are willing to dig into the system to expose them.

Not knowing or recognizing you have a problem is a fundamental issue if you want to drive a culture of improvement in your organization. In fact any attempt to change your system for the better will be difficult if problems remain ubiquitous and hidden, sometimes in plain sight.

> *"The clue is to be able to focus on what's truly important. Keep solving the right problems and solve them right so you won't have to return to them. In the end you'll be able to go much faster."*
>
> **– Jannes Smit, IT Director**

One practical and workable definition of a Problem is: "any performance other than desired performance at any given time." (Shook, 2008)[52]

You might think "but if this is the definition, then almost anything could be a problem!" And you'd be right. If we look for problems with this definition we'd probably find at least a hundred problems in your work today. The challenge is sorting out which problems to solve first by prioritizing the desired levels of performance. Some problems are good to be aware of, but they are not the most urgent ones. In that case we lower the desired performance level for the time being and focus on the ones that our team agrees on are the most pressing ones.

That's where exposing performance and specifying goals become useful. Being clear on how a problem affects performance or our goals helps set priorities, e.g. based on severity of the impact or urgency. If we found out there is a bug on our

---

* In some practices, problems are referred to as 'Impediments', they impede the flow of value. In this book we will use the word Problem and it is interchangeable with Impediment.

website that displays the wrong response after customers fill out a contact form, it may be less of a priority than the bug that generates the wrong price on our bike parts when customers do an online check-out.

Making problems visible

To be able to get better at what we do we must solve problems that are keeping us from achieving the desired performance. And to be able to tackle those problems, we must expose them by making them visible.

But therein lies one of the challenges with exposing problems. Teams that are used to working in an environment that has neglected problems for years on end are used to the impeded performance of processes they work with. As such they're no longer recognized as problems, but are accepted as 'status quo'.

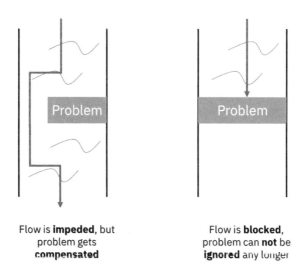

Flow is **impeded**, but problem gets **compensated**

Flow is **blocked**, problem can **not** be **ignored** any longer

Figure 3.20 – Problems tend to be compensated for

Visualizing problems in the Obeya helps us identify what we must versus what we can improve. It puts the exposed problems in the big picture that we see in the Obeya and as such helps us understand the context in which a problem occurs. This is an important step towards prioritization and effective problem resolution.

TIP - First, making an attempt to actually visualize problems is probably the most important step. Think carefully what problem you wish to solve in the visualization. Experiment with just one aspect of that problem. If you try to tackle more than one visualization problem at a time you are likely to find yourself with an ambiguous solution in the end. Your first attempts might not be brilliant, but it will be better to have any visual context rather than having none. The second step is to keep experimenting with it until you hit the sweet spot that will solve your problem. And then you keep improving as your needs for visualization are bound to change over time as your product delivery methods change or you learn and create need for new insights.

HOW TO APPLY THIS PRINCIPLE IN THE OBEYA

Another reason we're not applying continuous improvement in our work is because we haven't developed the habit for it. Mike Rother (2009)[53] has researched why organizations that copy the tools used by Toyota hardly ever seem to reach the same results. He came to the conclusion that adoption of tools is one thing, but more important is to create habits that include an improvement mindset. If we don't create habits, the tools we just purchased and played around with will end up in the shed and our garden will become overgrown.

Mike Rother has transformed improvement patterns into a very practical method with the same name that promotes the creation of a continuous improvement habit.

He analyzed the underlying pattern of behavior to understand Toyota's success, as he was curious why copying Toyota's tools wasn't bringing the expected results. It all boiled down to a certain pattern of thinking and acting that is consistent between leaders and team members, regardless of tools or seniority.

The great thing about this pattern is that it is accessible for everybody (starting at primary school) and helps create a new habit, both for people doing the hands-on work as well as individuals in a position to lead improvements and drive performance for their organization.

As Gene Kim, author of *The Phoenix Project* and the *DevOps Handbook* said about the Toyota Kata improvement pattern:[54] "this is the kind of thinking we would expect from any leader, certainly in about ten years from now".

Toyota Kata has the following characteristics:

- Applicable to any process or problem (that has no obvious answer);
- Short, regular intervals and experiments with gradual, visual and lasting results;
- There is a mentor (a leader), an improver (someone in the leader's team) that have a dialogue according to a set of standard questions on a coaching card;
- A second coach may be present that helps the Coach in learning the Coaching Kata;
- Regular, short intervals lead to continuous learning and small results every step of the way.

All parties learn, every session.

Let's see what the Toyota Kata improvement pattern looks like in our bike factory example:

	1. Get the direction or **challenge**	Before we try to go anywhere, we should make sure our efforts lead up to something that we believe is important. The Challenge is derived from the purpose in the Obeya. What is most important now? In The Bike Factory example a challenge could be to keep bike production costs below a certain amount of money to be able to compete on the market. A challenge should be ambitious, it's fine setting one for a year or so.
	2. Grasp the **current** condition	Before we can assess the best way to reach the challenge, we must first understand where we are today which will help us determine how far we are from where we want to be. Here are the (measurable, fact-based) conditions that result in the current production cost per bike. It's not enough to look at the total cost per bike, we must inspect the process to see what the conditions are that create that cost. For example the cost of materials, labor, transport, etc.
	3. Establish your **next target** condition	Now that we better understand the conditions for our cost challenge, we can determine which aspect of the cost we'd like to improve to reduce the over-all cost. Usually it will take a few next target conditions to end up where you want to be in the over-all challenge.
	Knowledge Treshold	In the types of challenges we take on with Kata, there will be things we don't know regarding our current or target conditions, that are valuable to uncover to be able to meet the challenge. Mike Rother calls anything beyond the knowledge threshold the 'mist of uncertainty'. This is the area where we're starting to make assumptions but we have to know for sure in order to be able to hit our target.
	4. **Experiment** towards the goal	Acknowledging that we cannot determine the outcome of our actions in the future, especially when entering uncharted territory, we should first start with experiments to widen our knowledge threshold and overcome obstacles on our way to the next target condition.

Table 3.1 – Steps of Toyota Kata improvement pattern

This pattern is followed in conjunction with the coaching Kata described under the Develop people principle. In the Cascade & Connect we see how this pattern evolves and runs through every level of your organization.

It is important to note that in the Obeya, when we start exposing problems we should be starting to see many potential improvements. This means you will have to make choices.

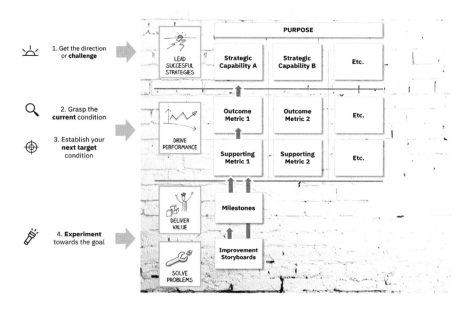

Figure 3.21 – Where we see elements of the Toyota Kata pattern when we 'zoom out' in the Obeya

TIP - If you have information in the areas of your Obeya, try and see if you can find how it relates to the challenge, the current condition and the target condition. If they don't relate, then how is the information adding value for the leadership team? Can they act upon it if necessary?

Cascade & Connect

It's great to get a leadership team started with Obeya. But the real value of improving a leadership system is only attainable when all teams are truly aligned with the same purpose and are able to act as one. So how do we connect your Obeya with the teams around you?

From CEO to operational level teams, everything is aligned. That is a difficult task to achieve, but we must start simply by consistent communication between the layers and departments in our organization. As such, a conversation is started from the top that is about three things:

1. Agreement on what it is we're trying to achieve;
2. Agreement on how to move forward;
3. Agreement on provisioning of the required support to get there.

Once the CEO agrees on these things with his or her team, his team can then relay that conversation with their own teams, who will relay it to their operational teams. On each level there is a handshake on the goals, the way forward and the support required to get there.

In a sense, the strategy flows through the organization. As such, when walking through a building visiting Obeyas on different levels, you'll recognize this cascade in the relay of purpose, Strategic Capabilities, items of the Deliver Value area, impediments that are raised, etc. Each Obeya may look slightly different, but if it sticks to applying the visual areas used in the Reference Model, it will have all the pieces of the puzzle and they will fit nicely together nicely.

What does this look like in practice? If the CEO walked past every leadership level starting from his own board level Obeya down to the work floor, he should see the same elements of his strategy throughout the organization, only more specific with every level. Each level further there is a deeper level of detail and understanding of how each part in the system contributes to the greater purpose. Being able to do this allows senior leaders to get a much better understanding of what is actually happening inside their organization, rather than looking at polished-up reports that have been interpreted and subjectively influenced so many times that they hardly have any meaning before they arrive at the boardroom.

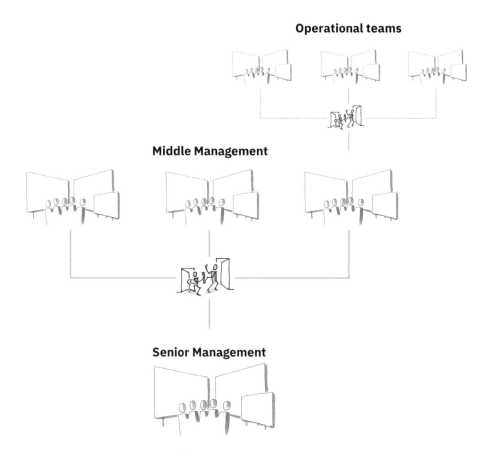

Figure 3.22 – Connecting teams on every level

We want to have this flow optimized so every team in our organization is aligned on every level towards achieving the overall purpose. How do we go from one level in the organization to the other?

GETTING TO THE RIGHT LEVEL RELEVANCY & GRANULARITY

Let's start with the information we expect to find in your Obeya and then move on to that of others. One of the hardest things to do in an Obeya is getting the right level of information on the wall and in the routines. Being able to drill down to what truly matters for yours is perhaps one of the most important skills a team has to learn while creating and maintaining their Obeya. It is important to realize that this whole process is in fact part of the learning for the team, and will probably never be finished.

So what are we looking for when choosing the right level of abstraction for visuals? The golden rule of Obeya abstraction: problems should be visible that are accountable up to the level of one team member and relevant to at least two others. If you cannot appoint a problem to one of the management team members, there's ambiguity in the information and you need to drill deeper. If the problem is not relevant for at least two other team members, the problem is too specific and should be addressed in a downstream area (the performance reflecting the problem should be visible nonetheless).

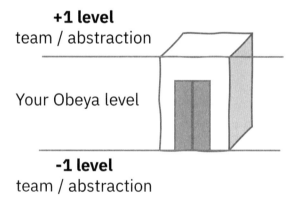

Figure 3.23 – Abstraction Elevator

DEPLOYING STRATEGY THROUGH DIALOGUE IN THE OBEYA

Each team on the next level in the organization will have to review the higher purpose and make an important consideration: "If that's the higher purpose, then what do we need to do and what do we need from the organization to make that happen?" That outcome should then be given back to the earlier team to be reflected on: do we understand each other correctly? Does this make sense in the broader perspective of what we're trying to achieve as an organization? By doing this we're essentially molding a purpose-driven ecosystem of teams that are engaged in vision, reflection and validation of the execution of strategy to achieve their purpose. And the Obeya is the arena in which all required context is created to make this happen.

Dialogue is extremely valuable in strategy deployment. It cannot be expected of a general to know the conditions on the ground of the operational squads. A leader in that position shouldn't base decisions on assumptions but rather learn from operational personnel to learn and understand the conditions and come up with suitable next actions in dialogue, with eyes on the ground.

David Marquet, in his book *Turn the Ship Around*[55] explains the effect on crew and performance when switching from "telling people what to do," to having people come up to you and explain what they intend to do in order to succeed in the mission of the crew. For this, he explains, people need clarity (on the vision) and competence (capabilities) to perform. Both are essential aspects for dialogue in the Obeya. Additionally, in his book he describes how, by shifting attitude and behavior towards leadership and responsibility, leadership grows through all levels of the organization, regardless of rank or function. That is one of the essential points in the Obeya, to enable and align leadership on every level of the organization.

Empowered operational teams

In essence, strategic decisions (policy) should be defined in such a way that they equip the operational teams to make situational decisions and support them act effectively. Strategic policy in this case could be: "We want to get to Rome as fast as we can but we want our route to be safe and we want to do it by foot." In many cases, there is no black or white answer on how to achieve just that. In this case the operational team makes a situational judgement that going through the forest best suits the strategic policy because the highway is not safe enough for pedestrians.

As they lead the way, they communicate their decision to the leadership in the back, informing them of the new developments at the front and how they have made situational decisions based on the policy. The leaders at the back are now aware of changing conditions for the teams ahead of them and also how teams are putting the strategic policy they created into practice. The essence of this story is, in order to execute any form of strategy, you need constant dialogue between all levels of your organization, constantly reflecting on strategic policy decisions that have been made and feedback on how and what is needed to have that put into practice. Fail to have this dialogue cascading through your organization and your strategy is likely little more than a paper exercise.

> *"A leadership team must understand what is it that teams need to be productive? They must understand 'our job as a leadership team is to create a great environment for the teams that deliver the value. Leaders should provide servant-leadership and trust that operational teams are capable of doing what they must do, or they will use the cascaded system to ask for support."*

– Sven Dill, Agile Coach

CATCH-BALL: CONNECTION AND REFLECTION

If one person tells a story to the other, that other person will tell it to the next just slightly differently. That's because the brain has processed the incoming information, put it into its own context, interprets the key elements of the story from that context and rephrases it using its own words to tell it to the next person. That happens at campfires but it also happens in daily business meetings.

Now a campfire group is fairly manageable, but in an organization with a hundred campfires this becomes more difficult. Messages are relayed every day in organizations, with limited and mostly non-verbal communication means, like email. Research indicates the major part of human communication to get a message across is non-verbal (McDermott, 1980) [56], so imagine the potential for misunderstanding if we keep using email as our primary means of communication.

There are many ways to promote connection and reflection, here are two practical suggestions in the Obeya:

1. Have people summarize decisions and their actions at the end of the meeting, verifying if everybody is on the same page in terms of expectations
2. Ask people to reflect on what is asked of them, translating it in their own words and context. Be open to dialogue to learn from their perspectives.

Figure 3.24 – Catch-ball using two-way conversation to make sure you're on the same page

POSITIONING - WHICH TEAMS COULD HAVE AN OBEYA?

Over the past five years I've helped start Obeyas for individual teams in lower and middle management, for programs, for start-ups and for board level management teams of big multinationals. All benefit from Obeya, as long as the systems thinking principle can be applied. That means that if there are three Obeyas with teams that are all trying to manage the same thing (overlap), there is probably overburden and waste, rather than benefit. Note that if this happens, it probably exposes the underlying problem that responsibilities are not clear within your organization.

At the same time, if you're a start-up with two or three people the Obeya can be the area where you apply your Lean Start-up techniques while monitoring your growth targets and aligning new teams.

In a large company it depends on how you are organized, but probably create one Obeya for every 200 to 300 people (so about twenty teams, more or less five managers). For start-ups this is different obviously, for them to start with an Obeya using Lean Startup metrics could be a very useful idea.

Part IV:
What's on the walls – five visual areas, eight hours a week

In Part III we learned about the principles for thinking and acting in the Obeya. They help the team develop and use the content on the walls in the Obeya. This helps them interact with their stakeholders, their teams and of course each other.

Now that we know why it's useful to work with Obeya and what the underlying principles are, it's finally time to look at the actual visual areas in the room. Obeyas come in different sizes, shapes and are likely to have different types of content. That's why it's not useful to discuss just one format in this book. We'll use the Reference Model as a reference for the visual areas. This relates every key responsibility of a leader to one visual area and related content in the Obeya.

Through this approach, it doesn't matter what your Obeya looks like or how you've positioned your areas, you'll always be able to relate its content to the Reference Model, helping you to check for completeness, consistency and navigate through any Obeya. But remember the systems thinking principle: all areas must be present to expose the workings of the whole system.

Five areas for each aspect of strategic leadership

Essentially, a leader has five key responsibilities which represent the fundamental work of a leader. It is not something on top of or next to other things. In the Obeya, these responsibilities are visualized.

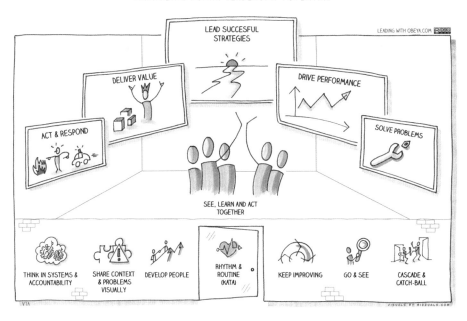

Figure 4.1 – Leading With Obeya – Reference Model visual areas in the room

The responsibility areas cover and support the exercise of common business practices any business school graduate would recognize like finance, marketing, risk management, process management, (project) portfolio management, etc. In the Obeya we try to illustrate these practices otherwise done in excel sheets and reports through lengthy, dusty meetings. We take the essential relevant parts of it and create a visually shared context with the team. As such, we support the team to actively engage in seeing, learning and acting together in these practices. Let's run through them briefly before discussing them further in the next chapters.

1. **Lead Successful Strategies** – The primary goal of a leader is to help the organization achieve its purpose. For this, a strategy that is best suited for the organization, given the circumstances, must be formulated, executed, tested and continuously improved. If a leader fails at this, the organization will not achieve its goals.

2. **Deliver Value** – Every organization delivers some kind of value to customers and or stakeholders. But we can only spend our money and our time once. A leader must be concerned with the selection of value that is being delivered in order to know whether it will fulfill customer and stakeholder needs. Ensuring maximum value is created is a key responsibility leadership will need to attend to. It's all about *doing the right things*.

3. **Drive Performance** – Not just the selection of, but also how value is being delivered is key to the success of the organization. If we don't improve our capabilities, things like delivery lead time or quality of our products and services will suffer. We must *do things right* in order to get the desired outcome and value for customers and stakeholders.

4. **Act & Respond –** Making a plan and making sure teams can get to work is one thing, but making sure they can then work without hassle or problems means leaders must constantly be available to Act & Respond to questions, requests, problems and new learnings that are uncovered on a daily basis on our path to glory.

5. **Solve problems –** In any organization there will be problems that have no obvious answer or solution. Recognizing them and actively identifying and working with teams to solve these problems is a key responsibility for leaders.

In the Reference Model you'll notice there is no specific order in which these areas follow, but they are on three levels. The top level is the area about strategy, which comes first because this defines the scope for the other areas. On the second level there are the value and performance areas, which go hand in hand, but depending on what kind of organization you are you might want to place more emphasis on one than the other (but never leave out one).

The Act & Respond and Solve Problems areas are filled with the logical consequence of the upper areas. As you're building your Obeya up in this order, you'll find actions and problems are logically exposed by addressing the upper areas. In this book we will explain each area in the order of the above list. If you follow the routines, you'll be able to run them and practice all aspects of strategic leadership with your leadership team each week, getting that part of your job done within eight hours. The rest is to deal with problems, do your administration, build relations and come up with improved strategic direction.

> **TIP** - Do these responsibilities make sense in your context? Is your team aligned and focused on these leadership responsibilities? If so, visualizing them and starting an Obeya to help you increase effectiveness as a team on these responsibilities is only a few steps away.

Two examples of Obeya layouts for two teams in The Bike Factory

To demonstrate the application of the Reference Model in practice, we'll provide some sample Obeya designs. The Reference Model helps identify the ingredients of any Obeya, but each room will have a different layout or emphasize different aspects that are most relevant to its team of users.

For example, for an Obeya for a team that has a strong focus on developing products, the team is likely to include much more of that product information and prototypes in the room than would be the case for a team that uses their Obeya to run the HR department.

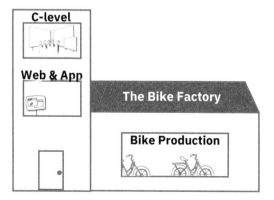

Figure 4.2 – The Bike Factory, a fictional case example

In this case we'll look at the example of a case that is used during the course of this book: The Bike Factory. This factory has two teams that deliver value in the form of a product (bike) and services (website and app) to customers. We'll look at a basic potential design for an Obeya for each of these teams. Both Obeyas are therefore related to the same overall organization. They may look different in layout, but they correspond to similar strategic aspects and are built up from the same elements of the Reference Model.

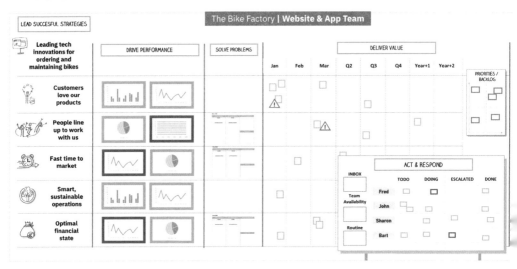

Figure 4.3 – The Website & App team Obeya

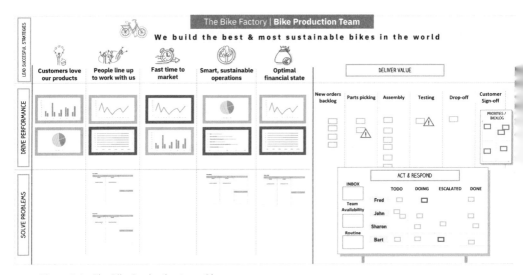

Figure 4.4 – The Bike Production team Obeya

This is more specific on what an Obeya might look like on a wall. Each of the areas contain different types of items like metrics, milestones, improvement storyboards, etc. Each type of organization might choose to add their own tools and methods in each area of the Reference Model. That is what makes it a versatile model, in essence the leadership responsibility areas remain the same, but how they are exercised and visualized is eventually up to the creativity and exploration of the team – what works best for them?

Do note that the Reference Framework's areas are setup in such a way that if you use different tools or ways of visualizing your strategy, managing work or exposing problems: feel free to apply it as you seem fit. The Reference Model suggests the visualizations and related activities a leadership team should perform, not which tools to use exactly and where they should be on the wall.

Before we move on to what is in the visual areas exactly in Part IV, let's start with understanding why we should make an effort to build an Obeya like this in the first place. Let's create some understanding on the problem before we try to fix it.

Again, there is no fixed prescription for an Obeya layout, these are just two examples. The key point is you should think carefully what is important to your team and then decide on a logical flow for the areas. Try it for six months and then evaluate and look for improvements.

> **TIP** - If you want to make sure everything fits on the area that you have in mind, or if you want to figure out how much physical area you need, try to make a sketch of the layout of the wall on paper. Another way to this is to take the actual A3 and A4 papers and temporarily put them on the wall to see how many fit next to each other to get a bit of a feeling for the size of the design. It is always useful to keep something like a tape measure at hand to mark the edges of the areas where you want to place separation lines.

Lead Successful Strategies

In a word of complexity, abundance of information and thousands of options to choose what to work on every single day for every single employee, we must be very clear in what we're trying to achieve with the organization. It is a requirement if we want to increase focus and avoid distractions and wasteful work.

The Lead Successful Strategies area is the starting point of your Obeya. It forms the foundation and structure for all the other areas in your room. In fact, every other visual should somehow be related to it, or it is likely not relevant.

The primary responsibility for any leader is to lead the organization towards the ultimate goal for existence: its purpose. Leadership responsibilities include (facilitating) the development of a winning strategy that sets out the overall movements and policies for the organization: what capabilities to develop, which products to invest in, how to create a future platform, how to position ourselves versus the competition, etc.

Creating and executing a strategic plan is not enough, we must know whether it is helping us achieve our goals. To truly lead strategy execution means engaging in a dialogue with key stakeholders, including teams, to address the organizational goals and connect them to a strategy that connects with people on both a logical and emotional level.

Only then can the strategy be understood and supported by these stakeholders. It is the job of a leader to make sure this happens and the Obeya provides an excellent physical context to have this conversation.

"You've got to think about big things while you're doing small things, so that all the small things go in the right direction."

– Alvin Toffler, Futurologist

VISIBLE COMPONENTS IN THIS AREA

Now let's see how this translates to components we'd like to see in the Lead Successful Strategies area. We expect to find visual evidence of this leadership team's intention to achieve their strategic goals. Remember, it helps us to see repeated messages of what's important so it sticks in our minds. That way it helps us make better decisions.

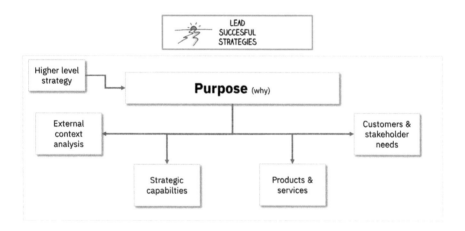

Figure 4.5 — Possible elements in Lead Successful Strategies

IT STARTS WITH WHY

In the Obeya, the purpose is what needs to be agreed upon first when a team gets started. It defines the success of the team and guides every action that follows for their own team as well as the teams they lead. It basically explains why to come to work every day. For the Prius, the first purpose was to "Build a car for the 21st century." That was the starting point for exploration that eventually lead to the Prius.[57]

It's worth spending some time on this with your team both for your own Obeya as well as for the process of cascading it to the teams you lead. Research shows people in organizations to become much more effective if they experience a sense of purpose and understand how their work contributes to that. (Buckingham, 1999)[58] Simon Sinek (2009) in his book *Start with Why*[59] explains how people identify with a purpose and how it binds them in terms of loyalty towards an organization and its products and services. If we look at it from the other angle, the lack of visibility or understanding of a shared purpose actually impacts the team's performance in a negative way (Lencioni, 2002)[60].

CREATING A PURPOSE

Let's start with defining it and putting it up in the Obeya as the first thing we do. A good purpose provides context for daily decisions to leaders, managers and operational employees.

Try to imagine you have the choice to work for two competing companies with the following purposes, which one would you rather work for:
A. "Our ultimate purpose is to inspire and develop children to think creatively, reason systematically and release their potential to shape their own future." (LEGO)
B. "We build plastic toys with which you can build things."

Purpose B. is fictional, but could represent a company creating similar products as LEGO. The key difference between the two is that the second one states the "what" we do, whereas the first one describes "why" we do it. And you notice the difference when reading B. Here the "what" is actually a determination and hence limitation of scope (to build plastic toys). But the statement of Lego invites everybody in the company and its stakeholders to put their efforts into something that is much bigger than building plastic toys – it is to positively affect the future of mankind. Needless to say this invites people to evaluate the meaning of their work quite differently.

There's more to a purpose than simply writing down what you do as a company. Here is a checklist of aspects for a purpose that you might want to use to verify the quality of your purpose definition. Above anything else, the purpose always addresses the "why." Whatever we do on a daily basis, it should be somehow contributing towards it.

Aspects of a good purpose:

- **Contextual**
  Provides the framework in which autonomous teams make decisions that lead to the higher goal. The team can review all their activities and check that they contribute to the purpose.
- **Connecting**
  Brings people to work together as a team, and if applicable is derived from the higher purpose of the organization, aligning individual teams to head in the same direction.
- **Inspiring**
  Something that makes people get out of bed in the morning and take pride in what they do.
- **Ambitious**
  Drives the need for self-development and continuous improvement.
- **Personal**
  The words used are chosen by the team and reflect their beliefs and culture.
- **Short**
  Though a purpose will be extracted into critical success factors, the purpose itself should be of high enough level that it fits in a short sentence. It's the key words that make it powerful.
- **Described as an end result**
  Start with the end in mind.

TIP - Creating a really good purpose statement is a skill. Don't hesitate to ask professionals or people in your organization with a talent for creative text writing to help you with defining a purpose. Though the wording should include close involvement with the team, you could consider writing the key words and the starting point of a sentence with your team, and then ask someone to propose a few improvements or alternative sentences that your team can choose from. This is likely to speed up your process if the team can't seem to come to a conclusion themselves.

IDENTIFYING THE STRATEGIC CAPABILITIES

If you want to achieve your purpose, you must make sure your organization is capable of achieving it. Now that we have the purpose and we know what our products are, we can start looking at what is key for our organization in terms of capabilities. We call these Strategic Capabilities, which can be defined as: "the resources and competences of an organization needed for it to survive and prosper." (Johnson et al, 2009)[61] By identifying them you start exposing key elements in the system you're supposed to lead.

Discussing the Strategic Capabilities facilitates a conversation on what should we really manage and what should we not manage. This sets the scene for unresolved or unaddressed responsibility issues within or outside of the team. If done well, the team members can link all of their daily activities and responsibilities to this structure. At the same time, anything that is done by the team that cannot be linked to a Strategic Capability can most likely be stopped, or you might have just identified a missing activity or responsibility.

Identifying your Strategic Capabilities is again part of creating context – what does your team believe is truly necessary to develop as a capability for your organization on their path to glory? Generally speaking, organizational systems consist of similar Strategic Capabilities, although the way they approach them is different. Below is a list of topics that could be a Strategic Capability to your organization:

| Customer Satisfaction | Quality | Security, Legal & Compliance | Information & Technology |

| Profit / Cost | Sustainability & Operations | Human Resources | Delivery & Time to Market |

Figure 4.6 — Topics commonly translated into Strategic Capabilities

This list is likely not an exhaustive list for your organization, or you might use different words or combinations. The list in this book is intended to help you identify potential topics for the legs of your table. Simply put, your team can select the topics they think are critical to achieving their purpose.

MECE: providing a solid foundation for your purpose

Think of it as the legs of a table. Your purpose determines the number and the quality of the legs that are required for a table. If your table has too few legs, it will become unstable and have no solid ground on which to achieve the Purpose. If your table has too many legs, they are redundant and make the table look odd and probably not easy to use, moreover, the redundant legs are a waste.

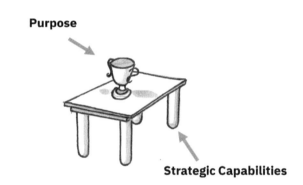

Figure 4.7 – Make sure you have the Strategic Capabilities to support your Purpose

To make sure you have the right number of legs for your table, apply the Mutually Exclusive and Collectively Exhaustive (MECE) principle for your Strategic Capabilities. That essentially means the complete set of Strategic Capabilities is tested on two things:

1. Each is a "thing" on its own (there is no overlap with others);
2. Together, they are a complete set (no key elements are missing).

As such, each Strategic Capability plays a key role to stabilize the table (your organizational system) so the purpose can be achieved.

Refining the Strategic Capabilities to suit your team

Selecting topics (either from the above list or your own) will be the starting point for the next step: qualitative statements for each topic by (members of) the team that describe the desired (target) state of the Strategic Capability as an end result. Essentially, the team will describe in their own words, what they think the required capability for the organization must be, preferably in one sentence.

Let's look at an example for the topic of customer satisfaction:
"Through dialogue, we know what our customers want and we deliver it to them. Feedback is continuously reviewed and translated into meaningful features that delight customers."

In our example you see the topic was discussed and elaborated upon by members of the team. The example looks fairly generic, but the important part is that the words are chosen by the team. They put together a qualitative statement that describes the desired state of the capability on this topic: what must we, as an organization, be capable of in terms of Customer Satisfaction if we want to achieve our purpose? The statement above is the answer to this question.

> **TIP** - There is no right or wrong for making Strategic Capability statements, they are your words and you choose how to position them under your table. Make sure your entire team is involved in creating the purpose, though refining the words for the Strategic Capabilities is usually something done by the people with that particular professional interest or by function (e.g. if you're the HR lead, you're likely to define the Strategic Capability that represents Human Resources).

On the next page is an example for The Bike Factory. The leadership team selected a number of Strategic Capabilities and formulated them in such a way that they describe what they think is needed to be successful as an organization.

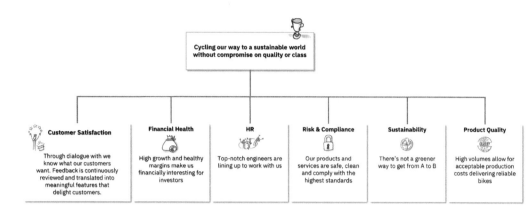

Figure 4.8 – Overview of the Strategic Capabilities that were chosen by The Bike Factory leadership team

For each of the Strategic Capabilities for The Bike Factory, there is a representative from the leadership team who is responsible for displaying the performance in that area. This person will also initially be responsible for driving the development of metrics and continuous improvement on their Strategic Pillar.

Here you can see a link to OKRs forming, as the Strategic Capabilities represent the high level categories in which Objectives will be defined that the team should work on in order to be succesful. At this stage, the Strategic Capabilities are just the umbrella as OKRs require Objectives to be set within a certain timeframe and Strategic Capabilities are an infinite inspiration for continuous improvement.

Since Strategic Capabilities are related to a certain subject matter, like HR or Security, you might find that if you've been inspired by Scaling Agile @ Spotify (Kniberg & Ivarsson, 2012)[62], the Chapter Leads are likely good candidates to represent the Strategic Capabilities.

Making sure that each Strategic Capability is formulated and represented by someone from the team is an important part of applying the 'think in systems and accountability'. Why? Each Strategic Capability represents a key part of the system that is responsible for reaching the purpose. If any part of that system fails, your table becomes unstable. Secondly, if we do see problems or challenges in that system, we want to be clear on who will be leading that challenge. And this is why a person should always be identifiable in relation to the pillars.

"Most people work on the same goal, but most of the time they're working on their own goals. In an Obeya they start realizing how it all comes together and then it starts to make sense."

– Nienke Alma, Agile Coach

TRANSLATING STRATEGIC CAPABILITIES TO MEANINGFUL DECISIONS AND ACTIVITIES

Now that we've defined a Strategic Capability for customer satisfaction, what do we do with it? How does a statement like that lead to meaningful decisions and actions in the Obeya?

First of all, it's useful to decide with your team who will be representing this Strategic Capability. This could be the sales director, the marketing lead in your team, or simply someone who's most interested in the topic if you do not have any particular segregation of duties in your team.

Let's break down the statement into its parts so we can see how it might lead to a more specific level of granularity that can lead to the discovery of metrics, policy and meaningful action in the Obeya.

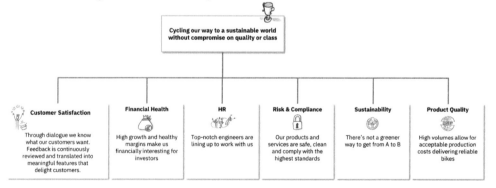

Figure 4.9 – Strategic Capabilities lead to relevant information gathering for other parts of the Obeya

As you can see in the above figure, a qualitative statement can provoke a number of questions or actions that we might not have an immediate answer to.

This is when we start building the bridge between Lead Successful Strategies and identifying metrics we will want to use in the Drive Performance area. Each of these metrics, since they are all related to the legs of the table, give us information that matters towards the Strategic Capability and hence achieving the Purpose.

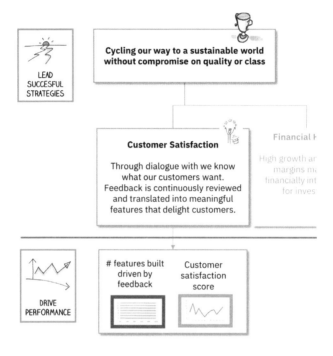

Figure 4.10 ─ Each Strategic Pillar helps identify potential metrics to be used in the 'Drive Performance' area

Providing these metrics may lead to new insights, decisions, developments, actions or experiments by the leadership team, for example:

- "Let's create a feedback functionality on our website to make it easy for customers to leave feedback on our products", or
- "Let's prioritize more customer-driven projects in our portfolio so we are actually providing them with what they want".

We have now formed the strategic fundament with our team:

1. The Purpose on our tabletop reminds us why we do the things we do.
2. The Strategic Pillars or legs of the table help us understand what we must do to be able to achieve that purpose and provide a solid foundation.
3. Each Strategic Pillar represents a key aspect of your system that should be

explored, uncovered and learned from. The metrics from the Drive Performance area will help create visibility on this.

You have now formed the basic fundament of your Obeya.

OTHER ELEMENTS YOU MIGHT WANT TO ADD IN THIS AREA

Depending on the needs of your team, you might want to extend the fundament with tools or other information that is relevant to you. Remember, the Reference Model is generic in the sense that if you use particular tools or ways of visualizing your strategy, then please use them however you see fit. Let's look at a few examples of other things you might want to put on the wall (non-exhaustive):

- **Customer & Stakeholder needs**
  A voice of the customer is a representation of the actual customers' needs and translates them into a guiding policy. Any team and organization will have some form of customer, user of their products and services or stakeholder of their organization. Customers can also be next-in-line customers, when multiple teams create or deliver parts of a product or service before something that is actually valuable reaches the end-customer. On the strategic level, it may be relevant and useful to identify and understand the general needs of customers, for example through the use of personas or real life people that represent groups of customers or stakeholders for you.

- **External analysis**
  By visualizing and sharing information about external developments in the Obeya we're trying to pick those aspects that matter and should (!) affect our decisions in the next quarter to year or so. One practical way of doing this is using the PESTLE analysis.[*] It might affect priorities in areas like Deliver Value where we choose which projects to prioritize, or it might affect choices such as using only recyclable materials for packaging instead of bubble plastics. In providing external contextual developments, the team shares and learns about the developments and can adjust their policy accordingly in the next period of time.

- **Overview of products & Services**
  On this level we try to identify those key products and/or services that are recognizable for our customers and/or stakeholders. Identifying them on this level helps position them and make decisions. It may very well be that each of those products or services are built up out of hundreds of sub products or services, but that's not the level we're looking for here.

---

[*] Stands for: Political, Economic, Socio-cultural, Technological, Legal & Environmental

> **TIP** - A business model canvas can be a useful tool to use at your Strategy area, since it addresses many of the starting points any leadership team will want to be on the same page when they run an organization together.

ROUTINE AT THIS AREA

Typically, the routine in this area happens as often as you need to review your strategic outline. Your annual leadership off-site is probably an ideal moment. That could be once a year or every half year,or whenever something happens that impacts your strategic decisions, like a reorganization or new CEO.

Since the nature of strategic sessions is usually to take a step back and change perspective from everyday operations to the bigger picture and larger outlook, it is useful to not try and cram your meeting about this area in a two-hour session.

Rather, take some time with your team to refresh your purpose and consolidate your learnings and insights. Take a day, maybe two, to go through the content, involving people from the teams you lead, your stakeholders or even a selection of customers, getting external inputs and recommendations and doing a workshop that lets you think outside your daily narratives.

> **TIP** - Prepare your meeting with an agenda, a goal for each point and timeboxes so your time is well spent. Strategy is something you can talk about forever, so ask for help from a facilitator or coach so you can focus on the content. Finally, make sure you have key information from your Obeya readily available. If possible, do it in your Obeya as all relevant in formation will be there. Taking a high resolution picture and projecting it on the wall often helps your teams spatial memory relate to the content on the walls of the Obeya even though they're not physically in the room.

Drive Performance

Driving the performance of your organization is only possible if you know where you want to go and if you know where you are today. Flooring the gas pedal of your car without knowing if the road is clear and if you're headed in the right direction is not something you want to do, unless, of course, that was the point of it.

In the Drive Performance area we will include the most important metrics that will help you steer your organization towards achieving its goals. It could be seen as the cockpit of your organization if it weren't for the absence of a windscreen through which you could see the actual road ahead. Therefore, the metrics in this area are primarily for exposing our system and learning from it, so we can identify and prioritize areas for improvement.

VISIBLE COMPONENTS IN THIS AREA

In this area we'll find a strong relation with the Strategic Capabilities identified in the Lead Successful Strategies area. They provide the basic outline for the metrics that we'll be creating in the Drive Performance area. We must create these metrics to learn to what extent we are capable of executing our strategy and meeting our objectives. So far, we have formulated the Strategic Capabilities as qualitative statements. As of now we will explore their meaning by adding definition, like: "let's measure customers satisfaction, but what does it mean and how do we do that exactly?" Answering these questions helps make the Strategic Capabilities come alive on a much more specific and meaningful level.

On the next page is an example of what the Drive Performance area might look like. As you can see, there is a clear link with the Strategic Capabilities. This layout helps visualize our strategic goals (the Strategic Capabilities), where we are today (Outcome Metrics) and what aspects impact that outcome (Supporting Metrics). Moreover, we apply color coding to help the team expose problems that they will need to respond to.

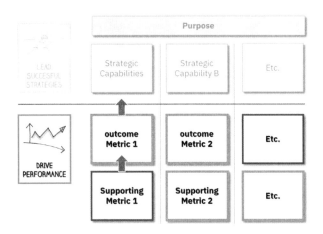

Figure 4.11 – Visible components of the Drive Performance area, red = act, green = within desirable limits

WHAT IS PERFORMANCE?

Performance basically tells us something about where we are in relation to our Strategic Capabilities and our capability to achieve our purpose. By improving the elements of the system we hope to improve the outcome towards our Strategic Capabilities. In doing so we are also structurally increasing the ability of our organization to achieve our goals faster, in the best possible way.

Driving performance also means we are better able to deliver the products and services in the Deliver Value area. How are they related? Imagine you have a blueprint to build the best car ever made, but you have absolutely no engineering expertise in your organization to build a car. Good luck with planning the delivery of that car. If you don't have the organizational capability to build it, you're likely to get nowhere with it anytime soon.

SELECTING METRICS FOR STRATEGIC CAPABILITIES

We can measure almost anything to some degree, but the relevancy and determination of the usefulness of that measurement depends on why we are measuring it. Just plainly picking a number and acting on it is like driving a car blindfolded and only using speed as a metric: though relevant for matching the speed of other traffic or reducing the impact of a collision if we go too fast, it is not the only metric we need to get to our destination.

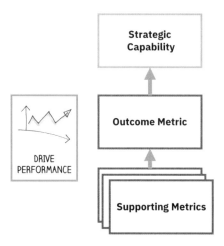

Figure 4.12 — Supporting & Outcome metrics

Outcome Metrics

Now that we've defined a qualitative statement for each Strategic Capability that will help us achieve our purpose, the next step is to find a way to see if we are able to actually increase our performance in relation to that Strategic Capability. We call these Outcome Metrics. They are a result of the way we do things and give us the (best known) indication of performance on a certain topic.

Outcome Metrics are often based on multiple constituent aspects we call supporting Metrics'. For example, the total monthly cost of our Bike Factory shop is the result of constituent elements that support the outcome towards the total monthly cost: rent, utility bills, cleaning and maintenance costs. Each is a different aspect of the Total Cost of Ownership (TCO) on a monthly basis for our Bike Factory shop.

In relation to OKRs, the outcome metrics are positioned under the umbrella of the Strategic Capabilities and both set your Objective (by setting a bar and aiming to achieve that within a certain timeframe) as well as measure your Key Results. They're the metrics that matter to understand where we are today and how we are doing towards achieving our Objectives.

A relatively easy example for a Strategic Capability related to financials is profit. In a very simple form it could be measured as follows:
Profit = (sales volume * commercial price in € – total expenses in €)

In this case, the Profit is the outcome towards our Strategic Capability as a result of its constituent metrics:

- Sales volume.
- Commercial price.
- Total expenses.

Outcome Metrics are often related to these three topics[63]:

- **Quality** (better bikes, First Time Right).
- **Cost** (lower production costs, higher profit margins).
- **Delivery** (fast time to market, no waste in the process).

Supporting Metrics

Digging deeper into the system is necessary in the search to reduce expenses. The leadership team of The Bike Factory wants to try and lower expenses by creating more bikes with the same amount of labor costs. This is where we start looking at metrics in processes that are on a deeper, more operational level in the system. Each process consists of (1) an input, and (2) a set of activities, that contribute value towards (3) an output.

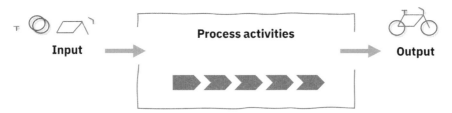

Figure 4.13 — Input, process output

The way this process is performed affects the outcome towards one or more of the Strategic Capabilities. For example, the duration of the process to create a bike affects how many bikes we can make with one production lane. If we pay € 100 a day to run the production line, but we can somehow produce twenty bikes instead of ten, the outcome is we are able to reduce our costs per bike on this aspect by 50%.

So Process Metrics tell us something about the conditions that are in place that are responsible for the current outcome, or result that we're getting towards our Strategic Capabilities. If we seek to create the right conditions to lower expenses of our bikes, the process metrics are one thing we must investigate to tell us more about those conditions. Once we understand the working of the process, we can make targeted changes to it in order to improve the conditions and get a better outcome towards lowering expenses.

In this case, there is a direct relation between the outcome (profit) and the underlying conditions (sales volume, commercial price and total expenses). The leadership team for The Bike Factory wants to have a high margin so they are attractive for investors. As such, they now have three knobs to turn in order to increase their profit: increase sales, increase the commercial price, or lower the expenses.

Leading and lagging

The Outcome Metric is can often be seen as a lagging metric: it is the result of something else, the outcome of things or events that happened earlier in the process. If we can identify these things, we can think of them as knobs that can be turned to change a certain Outcome such as cost, lead time or quality. Those knobs can then be referred to as leading metrics.

In the above example, the Outcome Metric is profit and the sales volume is the leading metric. If we turn a knob to raise the sales volume, our total profit is likely to rise. In order to do that, we should probably invest in things like marketing. Note that we should be careful making assumptions on how one metric affects the other. For example, we think raising the sales volume leads to a higher profit outcome, but it might also affect other parts of the system; marketing costs might rise or quality issues might start occurring in order to meet the demand which leads to negative promotion of the product. Eventually, it indirectly affects total expenses in a negative way, as well. That's why we should carefully monitor the movements in our system on a regular basis while testing our hypotheses and assumptions.

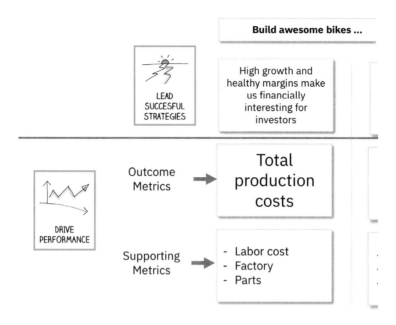

Figure 4.14 — Example of flow from Strategic Capability to Supporting Metrics

Identifying a threshold or target for performance

Once a metric is selected, we will be discovering what the behavior of that particular metric is. After a few instances of measurement, we will start to see a pattern of behavior or performance. The pattern may be somewhat static or erratic, but in any case it tells us something about the current performance. Sometimes this is called a baseline.

We can use a baseline to start learning about the behavior of the metric, but it will not help us drive performance. For that, we need to set a threshold that indicates a desired level of performance. By doing this, we are essentially identifying a charac-teristic of quality for this metric. Failure to identify performance thresholds (e.g. "if it operates within the threshold, we are satisfied with its performance at this point in time"), will mean it will be hard to reach consensus on what a problem is.

Identifying thresholds at the right level will help the team:
1. Identify problems instantly (wherever the thresholds are breached, the metric goes red).

2. Balance priorities (setting the threshold at acceptable levels means that sometimes we accept a lower performance by certain metrics that consequently turn green so we can focus on other metrics that are of higher importance).

Cascading through levels of metrics

Since the Strategic Capabilities are qualitative statements with wording chosen specifically by a team, they are largely unique for every other team. The Strategic Capabilities determine the metrics, and there is no standard set of metrics that should always be used on the Drive Performance area.

Below is an example of how the metrics on each level of The Bike Factory might look, from Strategic Capability (top) to how many minutes it takes to test a bike on the work floor.

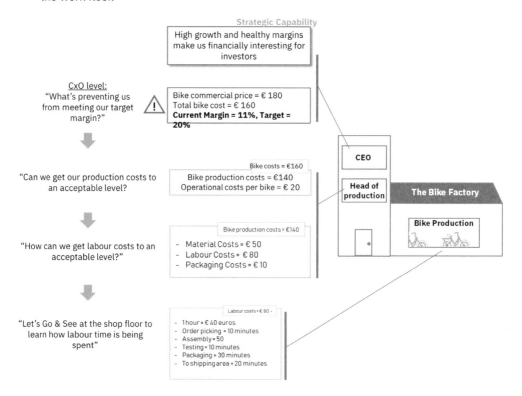

Figure 4.15 — Cascade from Strategic Capability to work floor operations

In the figure you first see the Strategic Capability that was established with The Board. In their Obeya session, they find that the margin on the bikes is not meeting the desired level. In order to understand and solve the problem, the head of production is able to provide more detail in her Obeya, where production costs are monitored. The major contributor to the production costs turns out to be labor cost. In order to understand why this aspect of the cost is so high, the head of production must visit the shop floor to understand how time is being spent per bike. Inspecting this process will reveal room for improvement.

This is a simplified example of a cascade in The Bike Factory case. The key point of this figure is to understand how profit margins that are discussed in the boardroom Obeya are eventually linked to how an engineer performs the activities of assembling a bike.

Bringing this back to OKRs, we saw that the Outcome Metrics are a suitable way of visualizing Objectives and Key Results. However, OKRs, like Obeya, work in a cascaded system throughout the organization. That effectively means that when we move our focus towards the work floor and Supporting Metrics, a new potential OKR on that level is exposed. Each Supporting Metric exposes a potential new OKR. For example to lower expenses in the production process of the bike may be a suitable OKR for the chief of the production engineers team. He or she may then create another OKR based on that for each team member and for each aspect of the production process.

Visualization of metrics

Metrics provide us with clues about our system; they help us identify what's important, where we can improve and where we'll find problems. To that end, metrics ought to be communicative, easy to interpret by the teams (and stakeholders), provide insights, learning, and above all, lead to actions or decisions you can make as a team. If you metric is there but it never leads to any actions for further development, decision-making or learning activity, then what is the added value of the metric?

The way you visualize your metric can go a long way towards the quality of interpretation by the team. Here are a few pointers that can help create well-visualized metrics. A good visual metric:

- Is neatly visualized and uses colors;
- Is contextual for one (management) level up and one level down;
- Shows the agreed (!) boundaries of 'normal' operation (minimum and/or maximum marker line), or has a space for where it is allowed to operate before it goes **red;**
- Has rules for if and when it should be discussed in case it is **red;**
- Shows historical performance to identify trends and patterns;
- Is generated automatically with the press of a button as much as possible;
- Is available digitally on a shared medium and physically always visible in the Obeya room;
- Has the name of the person that represents and/or creates the metric.

"Where there is fear, there will be wrong figures."

- W. Edwards Deming (1993)[64]

EXAMPLE METRIC FORMATS

Statistics is another field of expertise that many authors have written about. In the context of the Obeya we will provide some basic introduction. We do recommend you include people with some degree of statistical knowledge on your team.

To get you started, here are a few tools that might be useful in your Obeya. Use them to learn and expose your system, establish a current condition (sometimes called baseline) and set a target condition.

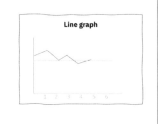	The line graph or run chart is pretty straight-forward and commonly used. Plots values on a timeline, exposing a trend, for example, of the output of a process. Can be used to identify behavior of a process and baseline its performance. By itself it does not provide enough information to determine action holders or where problems might be in the underlying system.

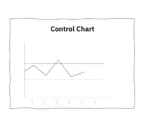	Originally developed by Shewhart, the Control chart is used to monitor the normal process boundaries of process performance and identify anomalies. Once a metric has been baselined and we know its normal mode of operations, we can set boundaries that tell is whether the process is operating within agreed limits. If it exceeds those limits it shows an exception, which might be the sign of a problem.
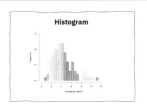	By analyzing occurrences over a timeline we are able to spot modality and outliers. If used to set a permanent baseline for performance, it can be used on the Performance Area, otherwise it can be used temporarily to expose a problem at the Solve Problems area.
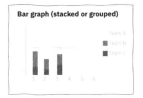	A stacked or grouped bar graph provides a value like the line graph, but includes the composition of that value by elements of that system, for example, which department has contributed how much towards the profit this month.
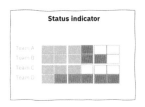	The status indicator provides a team overview with categories on the horizontal axis. Each team has a display of where it is at in terms of the categories, and what the status of that category is. It does not provide a trend but it is great in signaling statuses, for example, in Risk & Compliancy issues.
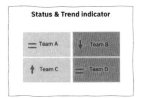	A basic indicator for each team on a particular topic which shows both a status regarding the threshold (red or green) and a trendline.
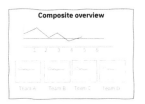	The composite overview can be useful when combining multiple visual metrics and displaying an overall status as well as component statuses, for example, performance at a team level. It allows for spotting both problems as well as pointing them out in the system. Multiple types of graphs and charts can be combined like this.

Table 4.1 – Visual tools to use in the Obeya

IDENTIFYING THE RIGHT METRICS IS PART OF THE LEARNING AND IMPROVEMENT PROCESS

For the leadership team, driving performance means being closely involved in translating the Strategic Capabilities into metrics and improvement challenges with their teams. The visual context that is created through this process should be the result of a continuous exploration of the system that produces the performance. Uncovering the Strategic Capability aspects of our system in the Lead Successful Strategies area was one thing, now we're going to learn how to impact them so we can increase performance of our system.

At every step of exploration, the leader is in dialogue with the people working in the system and uncovering new facts, information and knowledge. As this process continues, responsibility becomes clear, performance is made visible and, above all, the leadership team gets a better understanding of the system that produces results towards the overall objectives and purpose.

The dialogue facilitates a process that enables leaders to move beyond looking at reports for control, and firing commands towards operational teams. The evaluation of these metrics on each level of the organization is an example of the Cascade & Connect principle: they all connect.

Seeing metrics on a systems level can help identify potential bottlenecks or other problems in your organization. The metrics we find in this area may spark improvement projects or improvement Katas such as we can find in the Solve Problems area.

Red = an opportunity to learn and improve

What we want to see in this area is metrics that are red. Something goes red when it does not meet our acceptable threshold. Once we feel there are too few red signaled metrics, we should consider raising the bar for metrics that we think are important at that point in time. Why? Because that means we are actually raising the bar as an organization and trying to get better at what we do.

Once you have reached the stage where you are raising the threshold on metrics and raising the bar for your teams, you will realize that you have just taken a first and very important step in moving from firefighting mode towards continuous improvement!

But remember, we're not doing Management by Objectives. The most important thing we should always keep in mind when standing in front of the performance area is that it is not a means to steer towards results, it is a means to expose the system and to learn and improve our way to better results. A red indicator is not a trigger to start punishing people, it is an opportunity for learning and improving.

The moment we start punishing people for red signals is the moment the signals for improvement will start to disappear while the underlying system is still in trouble. Pushing for results rather than focusing our attention on creating an effective organizational system means we're Managing By Objectives and as we've seen in Part I that is not likely to get you lasting results.

METRICS: HANDLE WITH CARE

"The first rule of thumb is to be skeptical of all data."

– Kaoru Ishikawa, author of *What Is Total Quality Control – the Japanese Way*

As far back as the 1950's, people have warned about the risk of metrics being used as a tool to drive performance, while effectively driving output of those metrics — not a positive business outcome (Ridgeway, 1956).[65] As we've read in Part I of this book, complex systems should be respected as a whole, so we cannot pretend to understand and govern our organization based on just one or two metrics.

Metrics tend to steer behavior, which is one of the weaknesses in the way people tend to use Drucker's Management by Objectives: it leads to gaming the system to get a higher score on your KPI. But if the KPI isn't supportive of the greater goal of the system then you're optimizing only your own part, which is counter to what we're trying to do in the Obeya: systems thinking and cascading to make sure the organizational system as a whole becomes more effective.

But there are other pitfalls with metrics we should be aware of, and one of them is bias. Oversimplifying figures and numbers, finding evidence where there is none and probability fallacy are just a few biases discussed in Part I that play a big role in this area.

In his book *The Lean Startup,* Eric Ries (2013)[66] explains about "Vanity metrics" which are great for feel good (or bad) moments, but do not really tell you anything about how you are truly performing as an organization. For example, the number of registered users may be over one million, but if you have only a hundred active users that's not worth anything.

Bottom line: be careful when you use and communicate about metrics. Be honest about your intentions to learn and improve rather than use metrics for personal evaluation. Also, always respect the fact that a metric is a reflection of reality, it is not reality itself and the reflection might be distorted.

EXAMPLE ROUTINE

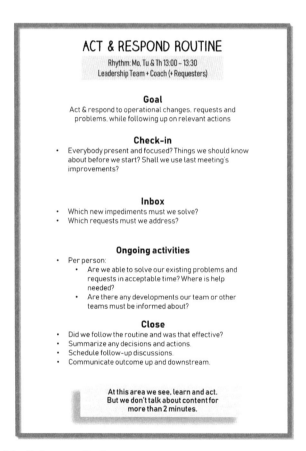

Figure 4.16 – Drive Performance Routine

Deliver Value

Delivery of value to our customers and stakeholders is key to living up to our purpose and, perhaps, even for our continuing existence. It is an essential task for leadership to ensure operational teams are able to deliver value to those we intend to deliver it to. This is why we must understand the value we intend to deliver and how it is delivered.

For The Bike Factory, the value that is delivered by the two teams we've identified is twofold: one delivers actual bikes from the shop floor, whereas the other sits in an office to develop new, cool features for customers to use on the website or app. But how do these teams ensure they maximize the value they deliver versus the time and money they put in? And how do they make sure that if one team starts the production of a new bike, the other team will make sure it is available on time on the website to be preordered by customers? We can't do it all at the same time, so we have to make choices.

A key task for anybody in a leadership position is to make choices regarding the delivery of value. This is often referred to as the practice of Portfolio Management, which can be defined as: the choices you make to utilize your limited resources in order to gain maximum value for (next in line) customers and towards your Strategic Capabilities. It is a practice every leader will have to master. Books and courses have been developed around the subject, it is taught at universities, entire departments have been tasked with it and it is sometimes embodied in the role of the Portfolio Manager or Product Owner in Agile movements. In this book we'll keep it short to understand how it relates to the Deliver Value area.

Essentially, there are two types of activities in this area that we will explain in the next paragraphs.

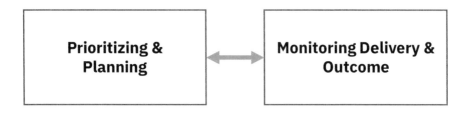

Figure 4.17 — Two aspects of Deliver Value

VISIBLE COMPONENTS IN THIS AREA

The following components should help visualize the work that's being done to deliver value as well as identify problems in the process of delivering value.

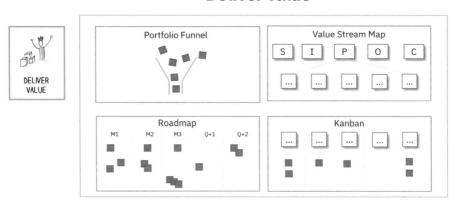

Figure 4.18 — Deliver Value potential components you could put on your wall

WHAT IS VALUE?

The delivery of value is about how we spend the time and resources available to us, to maximize value for customers and our organization. From that perspective, there are two ways of looking at value to be delivered:

1. Actual products and services to our external or next-in-line cus-
    tomers,* as well as the steps we take in the lifecycle** of those pro-
    ducts and services. In our bike factory, that means delivery of value
    would cover both the creation of a new production line so we can pro-
    duce our latest bike model, as well as how actual bikes are conse-
    quently built and delivered to paying customers. Some products are
    repetitive (always the same pre-defined product that is produced in
    a predictable fashion) and others are custom, like the creation of new
    and unique features on our website such as a visual color-picking tool
    in the ordering process.

2. The Change Initiatives we launch as a result of strategic choices.
    These initiatives are then expected to contribute towards one or
    more of the Strategic Capabilities of our organization. These kind of
    initiatives may be run through projects or programs. Examples may
    include: reorganization for cost saving, Lean or Agile transformations
    for quality increase and cultural change, outsourcing for focus on core
    competencies, projects driven by legislation changes, etc. The outco-
    me of each should increase the organization's capability to achieve its
    strategic goals.

Let's make this a bit more tangible through the example of our bike factory.

You can only spend your money and time once, and the constraints of the spacetime
continuum are unfortunately preventing us from doing it all at the same time. Let's
look at the key practices for prioritizing & planning value in the Obeya.

---

*   A next-in-line customer can be another team or department within your organization that you're delivering (partial)
services or products to before they eventually lead up to something an actual customer from outside your organization uses it.
**   A typical lifecycle includes the following stages: Definition, Design, Development or Implementation, Use or Deliver and
then either disposal, recycle or decommission, or back to definition for a next (iteration of the) product or service.

Product The bike produced at the factory.	**Service** The website on which customers can order bikes.
Product lifecycle A single bike is ordered, produced, delivered, used by the customer and collected for recycling once it is worn. **Production Lifecycle** Following the design of the bike as a product, we design the production process steps, machinery, supplier products, etc. in which bikes will be assembled and readied for delivery to customers.	**Service Lifecycle** A new feature could be built on our website which allows customers to select a certain color of bike. This feature will be designed, developed and tested and then implemented on our live website.
Change Initiative example A We decide to add "the bike of the future" to our product portfolio, which requires that we create a new assembly line, make changes to our website, contract new suppliers that provide batteries and electrical engines and train our people in the new technology. The Strategic Capability impact should be that we attract more customers and achieve a higher profit margin through this unique product. We intend to complete these activities in a year from now.	**Change Initiative example B** We decide to outsource the IT infrastructure department that manages the servers that run our website. This is a project of eight months to complete and requires we do a tender, change our processes, train people in supplier management capabilities and make changes to our website. The impact in terms of Strategic Capabilities should be a higher up-time (service quality) of our website and lower maintenance costs.

Table 4.2 — Differences between Products and Services

Creating context for prioritization with a feasibility matrix

You can use a feasibility matrix in your Obeya to have the discussion in your team on what's important and what's not. There's no science to this but it's a great tool for sharing context with your team and positioning your Change Initiatives. The idea is to estimate the initiatives based on their value towards the Strategic Capabilities or higher level strategic choices. Value is estimated both on the positive impact on the Strategic Capabilities (e.g. increasing customer satisfaction), as well as the urgency or cost of delay, for example, in case of compliancy issues (if we don't adhere to the new legislation before the January 1st, we might face penalties), or postponing the launch of a new product which means a delay in income.

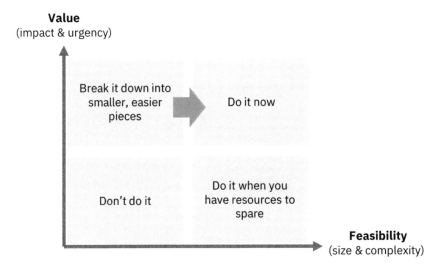

Figure 4.19 — Feasibility matrix for prioritizing value to be delivered

The simplest way is to use sticky notes for each initiative and consolidate it to a list that is then the priority for the next period. An Important aspect is to make sure the Change Initiatives are broken down in to digestible pieces that are sufficiently feasible so as to avoid the creation of "oil tanker" programs in which we lose all sense of agility and learning.

Needless to say, this activity should be done with a proper understanding or better, involvement of customers and stakeholders to provide your team with high quality contexts, avoiding assumptions and working with all relevant information to make choices in relation to value.

Product Owners can take the outcome of the Feasibility list to their Product Backlog; program managers can include in in their next iteration or program phase. If we do this exercise together, then we all align our efforts and consequently increase our impact.

Planning the delivery of value

Planning is basically an intention to unfold a series of activities in such a way that they deliver maximum value. We do this based on assumptions about the future and about the work we think is needed to achieve certain business outcomes. But the truth is, we never know what tomorrow brings. All is fine as long as we keep that in mind.

"Plans are things that change."

– Fujio Cho, Chairman of Toyota

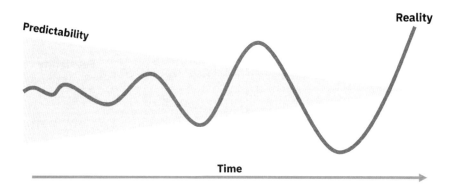

Figure 4.20 — *The further into the future, the less predictable the outcome*

ROADMAP

One form of planning is to create a high level roadmap for the Change Initiatives we tend to deploy that we believe will help us on our path to glory. This is usually an overview of work for at least the next year or years. A roadmap should not be considered a detailed plan of the future truth. It should be considered a means of communication to share context with our teams and stakeholders upon which they can consequently commit their efforts make choices on how to combine their efforts for maximum effect. This promotes alignment of activities and avoids waste of people working on different priorities and finding out later they do not add up, or worse turn out to be counterproductive.

In this context of the roadmap we explain the choices we make in terms of which turns we take and in which order to achieve our purpose. A roadmap consists of milestones relevant to our team, which represent intended achievements towards our Strategic Capabilities or Products and Services.

The items on a roadmap are usually high level and not planned in detail. The farther ahead in the future, the less time we should spend on detailed planning. Agile planning is great when there are less dependencies, and the roadmap should never overrule Agile planning principles. But some teams have to deal with the truth of fixed elements, such as a marketing campaign to go live on a specific date or a date in which certain legislation must be implemented. As such, a Roadmap is an important and useful means to communicate the work our organization intends to do with internal and external stakeholders.

PORTFOLIO

Once the planned activities are in the near(er) future, we have to start making choices on how we will actually spend our limited resources. As such, it would be good to refine the work to be done to a level where we can fit it in sizable chunks to free slots available for the operational teams that actually do the work. This allows the leadership team to engage in a dialogue with operational teams that consequently pull the work into the work slots for the next period. Once that process is ready, we end up with an overview of what activities we will be spending our time on in the next period and how it all adds up. This should be the best possible way to deliver value both within and outside the scope of our department.

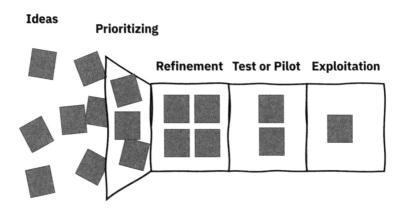

Figure 4.21 – Basic example of a portfolio funnel

The concept of a portfolio funnel is used to limit the amount of work in progress, starting from many ideas, and then drilling down in each phase to smaller selections that the team believes truly add value for the organization, its customers and its strategic goals. The challenge with this practice is that ideas are hard to compare and estimate in terms of cost, benefit, lead-time and effort. For that reason, using the feasibility matrix as a starting point, refining and picking potentially viable and valuable projects on a work list and limiting the work in progress for each phase of the portfolio funnel in a Kanban-like fashion, is a simple yet effective way of prioritizing work.

Dealing with dependencies

In order to make smart decisions on what to prioritize through capacity planning, we must understand from a broader perspective where the key dependencies are. The first step to take when minimizing dependencies is to make sure the composition of teams is done in such a way that they are multi-disciplined and have a large amount of autonomy over their (part of the) product.

Secondly, we want to minimize the amount of dependencies we display in the Obeya. Why? Because managing dependencies in itself is not a value-adding task. Visualizing and documenting many dependencies inevitably leads to waste.

Operational teams and people in roles such as architects need to identify dependencies that remain outside the team and make sure they align with the other teams in terms of planning. The primary role for management of dependencies should be with the operational team. Once it comes down to making more strategic decisions on dependencies across teams, the leadership team should facilitate this conversation in close involvement with the operational teams.

The dependencies that arise in that session are relevant for the strategy in the bigger context over multiple internal and possibly external teams. That is the only kind of dependency you would want to visualize in your Obeya. As a result, we can start to create a pull system where changes are worked upon as they are needed, rather than pushed, and sitting there waiting until they can be used.

Example milestone card

As we know, in the Obeya the areas are all related to each other. As such, a milestone should contain information related to its strategic value as well as its impact on the Drive Performance area, along with some other pieces of information that are relevant to the delivery of value. Each organization has their own ways of planning things and might want to change the wording or add and remove fields.

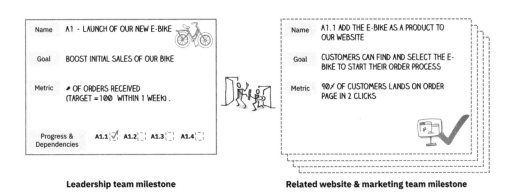

Leadership team milestone   **Related website & marketing team milestone**

Figure 4.22 — Milestone templates for two levels of abstraction

TIP - The first time a team puts up their portfolio wall, they will find all their projects visually displayed on the wall. Experience teaches that this can be quite overwhelming, especially if the organization is not used to active management of their portfolio. Problems that might be exposed right away:

- There are multiple top priority projects (but there can be only one! Otherwise it's called grouping, not prioritizing).
- People are unsure whether this actually encompasses all of the active projects.
- It is not really clear what, by definition is a project, a change, a small project, etc.
- It is simply an overload of information that seems poorly structured (e.g. having over a hundred projects visually displayed out of the blue will likely be overwhelming).
- The management of all of these projects might seem extremely complex due to variability in how they're managed, and visible (or invisible) dependencies between them.

Make sure you don't get discouraged. Don't let anybody tell you the visualization doesn't work because what you see does not make sense. It is, in fact, the exposure of problems that might be scary. Be bold and take them on, one at a time. Things can only get better from here.

MANAGING DELIVERY & OUTCOME

Pulling value through your delivery funnel

Once we've committed to spend our resources and have an estimate of the work to be done we can start doing it. Teams estimate their available capacity based on empirical data, for example how many bikes have we been able to produce under the same conditions during the last period? Or how long does it usually take to produce a feature for our website of this size and complexity?

As a rule, when teams are pushed over their available capacity by deadlines given to them by leadership or customers, they will go slower without a doubt. Teams know best what they are capable of and should be responsible for planning of their own work. Leadership should not push work but rather provide strategic guidance, help translate stakeholder needs and support teams in effective planning and execution of their work.

Identifying your value streams

The process which delivers products or services is referred to as a Value Stream. In order to see how this process of value creation works, see the Value Stream Map (VSM).* A Value Stream Map is a tool used to examine and investigate a process with the purpose of improving it. But it starts with the actual exposure of the key processes in your organization that we as a leadership team are responsible for.

The VSM provides context for the team: how does our process work? It also identifies problems and sets an improved target condition for the process. The intent is to improve the lead-time, quality and cost of the value creation process.

As we've learned in Part II on creating visual context, it is crucial to do Value Stream Mapping and the related improvement efforts with the team to achieve the necessary context in which people operate on a day to day basis.

Bicycle Factory value streams on different levels

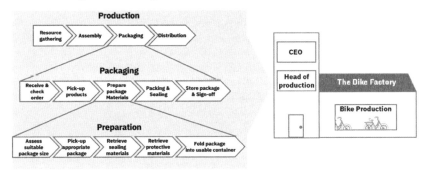

Figure 4.23 — Example value stream on three levels of the organization

---

*   Some quality books have written on just this topic, like M. Rother & J. Shook, 1998, Learning to See: Value Stream Mapping to Add Value and Eliminate Muda. In Leading With Obeya we'll keep the theory to the bare minimum.

The value stream is essentially the series of activities on a certain level of abstraction that lead up to the creation of value for (next in line) customers. It is valuable for leaders to understand the value stream, as the way it is designed should determine the baseline for how it is executed in practice. If we see deviations from the design, it probably exposes a problem either with the design or our ability as an organization to execute it accordingly. Also, it will help leaders isolate problems to a particular part of the value stream, as the execution of each step of a value stream will impact Strategic Capabilities such as Quality, Cost or Delivery.

Let's look at an example for The Bike Factory below, which displays the Packaging value stream.

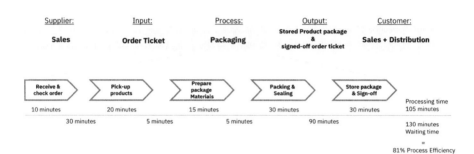

Figure 4.24 — Using VSM to analyze the process performance

From the example we can derive information about the process, including its input, output, the customer, the lead time and also how much waiting time between steps is involved. We can combine this with performance related information like:
- # of packages processed;
- # of packages causing delays;
- # of rework in case of wrong packaging;
- # of complaints by customers related packaging;
- Etc.

Providing both the map and the data, we would be able to involve representatives from leadership and work floor to share context and investigate step by step where in the process we can find potential problems and start solving them. This is much more effective than blindly troubleshooting process, related issues and hoping for better outcomes.

TIP - The likely bias you might experience by looking at this Value Stream example is that it seems easy to create a value stream map like this, and that it looks so obvious that you won't even have to bother making one because anybody can come up with something that looks so easy. After all, everybody knows already how the processes in your organization run, right?

Here are a few surprises that usually turn up when creating value stream maps, that make it a valuable exercise in spite of what a biased brain might think:

1. People appear to have different ideas on how the process really works.
2. A lot of problems are caused by unclear definition of input, output or who the customer really is.
3. Teams are focused on their own activities, rather than optimizing the lead time for the entire value stream.
4. Unless you've adopted Continuous Improvement for a while now, your process efficiency is likely to be below 10%.

Making a VSM is not for fun, it will expose waste in your key processes very easily so that you can start improving your organizational system.

PREPARING FOR A DELIVER VALUE SESSION (EXAMPLE SCENARIO)

Roy is preparing his first Deliver Value session for The Bike Factory. He is new to the team and was given the request by the senior manager to make a proper representation of where his team is at in realizing a part of the new product platform. Wanting to make a good impression in his next portfolio wall meeting, Roy decides to chat with the facilitator about the expectations of the meeting. The facilitator explains the routine for the meeting and the topics that have been discussed recently. He also offers to help use the templates for the portfolio wall cards and put them on the wall correctly. Roy then goes to his team leaders and discussed the key features they are working on for the shared platform and their status, while drawing the outline on a whiteboard with Post-its. The team leaders points to it, showing they're progressing as expected and help Roy with formulating the notable events since the last portfolio meeting and anything important for the next week. Then one of the team leaders raises an issue. Some of his people still don't have access to the system they need to work on. He claims this issue has been outstanding for a few weeks and if not resolved in the next week there will be delays in one of the key features. Since the features are now on the whiteboard one of the other team leaders indicates that if the first one is late then one of their features will also shift in time, having consequences for customers and potentially business results.

Roy takes a snapshot of the whiteboard after having marked the issue of the system access to the related feature on the board. He then goes back to the facilitator to make sure the features on the upper level board are in the right place and the problem of one of his team leaders is visible. The facilitator help place a danger magnet at the particular feature and recommends Roy prepare an 'impediment' template for the senior management portfolio level meeting the next day. As Roy fills out the template for raising an impediment he realizes he forgot to ask the root cause and how his team leader wants to approach solving the situation. After having spoken to the team leader at the end of the day about the missing pieces for addressing the problem, Roy feels he's well prepared and ready for the portfolio wall meeting the following morning.

The next day, as the meeting starts, Roy is the first to address his impediment. He explains to the group where the problem is by pointing it out on the board, while stressing the urgency by outlining the potential impact on their plans. He also relays the root cause, followed by nodding of his fellow team members as they recognize signals to this problem affecting their own teams as well. Roy requests with one of his fellow senior leader team members to advance the development of an access control feature scheduled in two weeks on another lane of the portfolio wall, so to prevent these problems in the future. Roy's colleague acknowledges the issue and agrees to confirm the advancement of the access control solution by next meeting. The team now has a shared context of where Roy stands in his part for achieving their shared goals. They know he has a problem that has to be addressed and resolved at their level and what consequences this has on their shared portfolio. Moreover, the problem identified is relevant on a system level as more people appear to be affected by it.

EXAMPLE ROUTINE

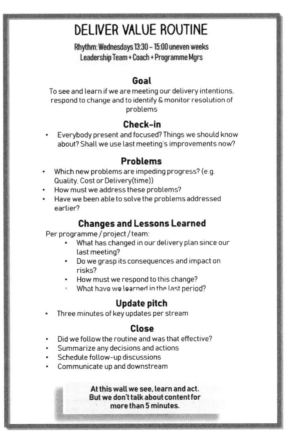

Figure 4.25 – Deliver Value Routine

Act & Respond

Usually having the highest frequency of meetings in the room, this area is a driver for progression, fast identification of problems and context sharing for follow-up actions coming from up- or downstream. Indeed it is also the closest thing for managers to what any Agile or Lean team already knows to be a stand-up.

Like in any normal team that embarks on the journey towards Lean or Agile working, the stand-up at first seems like a lot of meetings. However, remember that this time *is* the work and should replace existing meetings. There is no extra time, only more effective use of time. Moreover, teams will always be able to address their pressing issues with your leadership team, without having to wait longer than two workdays for a next decision-making meeting.

VISIBLE COMPONENTS OF THIS AREA

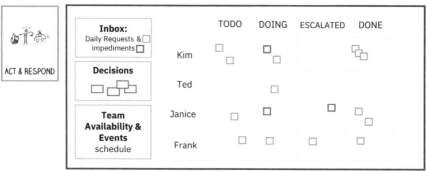

Figure 4.26 - *Act & Respond visual components*

Inbox

This is where any requests are placed before the meeting. The requests come from team members, operational teams or more senior level teams. Each request should be introduced during the meeting by someone who is capable of explaining the context of the request. This is to avoid making assumptions on what is requested and why. Also, the use of a template with certain fields like "what is the impact" or "why is it urgent or important now," will help the team make a decision on whether to address it immediately, or schedule it for later. This makes it more likely the team is able to respond appropriately.

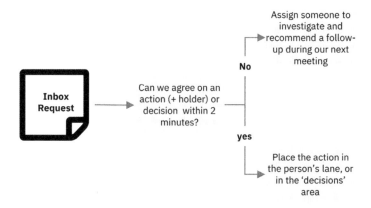

Figure 4.27 — What to do with inbox requests

Action board (Kanban/Scrum board)

On this board there is a simple To Do, Doing, Done structure for the activities of the team that are relevant to at least two other team members.

Most team members are likely to have worked with this kind of visual leadership system before, as more and more teams are adopting Agile practices.

The thing to manage in this area is agreeing on a definition of done; this to avoid debate on when something is finished. For example: "we've put an action on that impediment so we may now close the impediment" is a great sign of trigger-happy trouble-shooting: we shoot a solution at a problem and it disappears. The issue is,

179

you don't know for a fact the action (which we hope holds the solution) will actually solve the problem. Moreover, if we haven't investigated why this problem occurred in the first place we might need to spend time on it again in the future.

Impediments

If an impediment matters and we want to make sure it is actively worked on and solved, we will be able to track the activities related to an impediment on the action board. It helps if those activities are visually related to an impediment, for example by placing the actual impediment in your lane in To Do, Doing or Done.

> *"The strength of the Obeya comes not only from one room but rather a connection of the different levels of the organization to cascade messages up and down to help teams solve impediments that they're not able to solve themselves."*
>
> **– Sven Dill, Agile Coach**

Team availability & Events calendar

This shows any major events like company or tribe meetings, as well as holidays of team members or their regular part-time days.

TIP - Place this board on a mobile whiteboard if you can. That way you have the flexibility to have your stand-up in different locations or parts of the room if other areas are in use by other people. This provides more flexibility and access to information in the Obeya for others.

PRACTICAL EXAMPLE OF AN ACT & RESPOND SESSION

The team meets at the action board on Monday after lunch...

John opens the meeting "OK everybody, are we ready to start? Is everybody focused?" – people put away their phones and focus their attention.

John briefly explains the purpose of the meeting and checks whether the visuals have been updated so that the team is looking at the latest version of the truth of their system.

"Now let's start with the impediments", John says. To which Anne excitedly replies "Yes, I've got one!"

Anne waves around the impediment card she's just filled out and explains it to the team: "My team is trying to get the system live, but they are still waiting for authorization. It's been five workdays now. The impact of this is that marketing might need to postpone their campaign if we don't get it live within another two days. The root cause as far as I've been able to establish is a failure in the onboarding process where the engineers in my team were not given the appropriate system access," and we can't seem to fix this ourselves.

Anne continues: "John, is there any way we can get early access for my team?" John replies: "This seems important. I'll put an action on the action board to check with the guys to find the request and see if we can prioritize it for today."

He continues: "Do note that we've been very busy processing all kinds of access requests, especially since the new onboarding process has been in place." Anne says "yes, that was my feeling as well, perhaps that's where we'll find a root cause for this problem?"

Judy, owner of the onboarding process now joins the discussion: "The onboarding process should speed up productivity for engineers. It sounds like it's not doing that, but I also don't understand why because whatever we seem to do the access rights keep posing problems."

Judy continues: "There doesn't seem to be a simple solution, and we don't have all the data we need right here to make a decision, so I'll start an improvement in the improvement area on this and keep both Ann and John informed on our progress."

They close the discussion by putting John's action on the action board to be followed up in next stand-up, and taking a Kata template for the improvement for Judy.

EXAMPLE ROUTINE

Figure 4.28 – Act & Respond Routine

Solve Problems

The leadership responsibility for solving problems is visualized in this area. It helps identify problems, prioritize them, follow-up on solving them and help with applying the improvement mindset. By solving problems, we improve our performance towards achieving our goals.

Contrary to classical management beliefs, where problems are things to get rid of as soon as possible as they are in the way of our objectives, in this area we look at problems as the work we are doing to increase the performance of our system. By working on these problems systematically, we effectively increase the performance of the system. Hence, in the Obeya this area should show that our leadership team takes problems and therefore performance improvement seriously. We expect to find evidence of relevant, prioritized problem solving activities here.

> *"Working with Obeya helped us make it possible to quickly inform each other on problems, act upon and solve them. This actually prevents emails, and spending time on defining a structure, since there already is one. Effectively, this helps focus your time on solving the problem, instead of spending time organizing meetings and such."*
>
> **– Pauline van Brakel, Chief Product Officer**

VISUAL COMPONENTS IN THIS AREA

Although problems should be exposed in a visual way everywhere in the Obeya where they are found, this area specifically relates to the structural process of problem solving. That means if problems are small enough to be fixed with a simple action, they will go onto the action board. But if problems require more than just a few actions to be understood and solved, the Solve Problems area is the place to be.

The Solve Problems area is best suited to a place where the problems that are being tackled are logically related to the performance that must be improved. As such, we can make sure the problems we're working on are related to our ability to achieve our purpose. This helps prioritizing. For example, if a Strategic Capability is marked with a red status, we should be able to find an Improvement Storyboard in the related area quickly to get the performance up to the desired level.

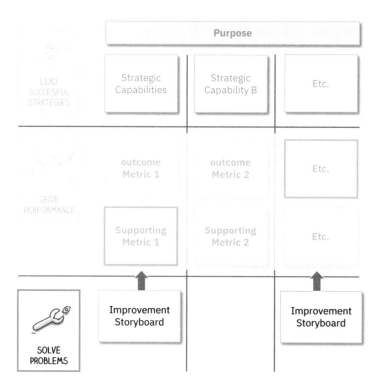

Figure 4.29 — Solve Problems area related to Drive Performance metrics that expose structural problems

Although you're free to use any kind of problem solving method in this area, we have a strong preference for using Improvement Kata in this area. The reason being that it is a fairly easy method to start practicing, though hard to master.

Addressing problems in the right area

Problems can be addressed in all areas and routines of the Obeya. But depending on their nature, we follow-up on them in different ways. The reason for this being that some problems are fairly easy to solve with just one or two actions that we could place on the Act & Respond board, while others remain too complicated to be able to remove their root cause with a simple action.

To simplify the approach as to what to do with a problem, here is a flow which supports the placement and resolution approach to problems, no matter where or when they are addressed in the Obeya.

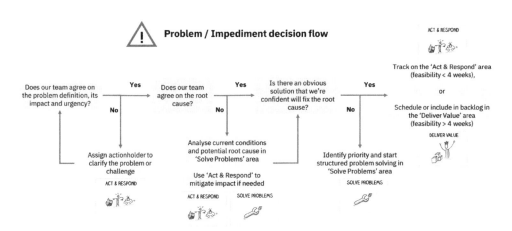

Figure 4.30 – Problem decision flow

Make sure you understand the problem and its context to avoid waste

A critical step in the problem definition flow we see here is the very first one "Does our team agree on the problem definition, its impact and urgency?". This is where our System 1 and biased thinking are potentially cause of wasteful action. Because if we make assumptions in this step, we might end up finding solutions to a symptom rather than a problem. The key message in any effective problem solving method that has been described is to make sure you truly understand the problem before you attempt to fix it. In his book Managing to Learn, John Shook (2008)[67] provides very insightful examples of what can go wrong between a manager and somebody in their team when they jump to conclusions about a problem. A simple yet effective way of avoiding issues with your problem definition at the start is to use the 'five times why' method: why is this a problem? By repeatedly asking that question the dialogue between the problem solver and manager is guided to deeper levels of understanding of their system and how one thing impacts the other.

STORYBOARDS FOR PROBLEMS WITH NO OBVIOUS SOLUTION

The improvement pattern and the coaching Kata are exercised at the Solve Problems area. They are visualized by using Storyboards, usually printed on a paper the size of an A3 (29,7 x 24 cm or circa 17.5 x 11.5 inches).

Just improving anything is not a good practice in Lean. If you spend time on one improvement, whereas another improvement has more impact on the customer and is of more urgency, the improvement could be considered a waste or at least not maximizing value add.

Also, when people know that their work matters it makes them want to work more because it has meaning. As we learn from Daniel Pink (2009)[68] having a meaningful purpose is perhaps one of the biggest motivators. But to achieve a sense of meaning, it must be very clear to people in the Obeya how the improvements that they spend their time on support the realization of the strategic business goals.

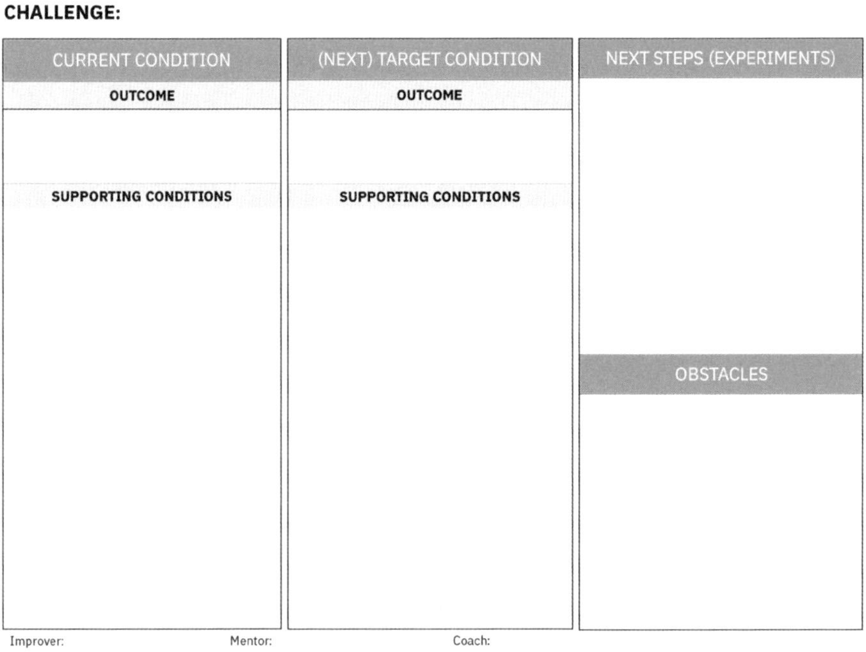

CHALLENGE:

CURRENT CONDITION	(NEXT) TARGET CONDITION	NEXT STEPS (EXPERIMENTS)
OUTCOME	OUTCOME	
SUPPORTING CONDITIONS	SUPPORTING CONDITIONS	
		OBSTACLES

Improver: Mentor: Coach:

Figure 4.31 - Improvement Kata Storyboard example

You need skills and tools to effectively solve problems

Albeit for a (relatively) simple or more complex problem, in any case the persons working on it will greatly benefit from having learned and practiced problem solving techniques that help expose the system in which the problem occurs, dig down to the root cause and make improvements on a systems level rather than a superficial symptoms level. Do not underestimate how much more effective a person can be at identifying current and target conditions or coming up with highly effective experiments if they master these tools and techniques. And do not underestimate the potential of such a person teaching those tools and techniques to their colleagues who can then teach them to others.

Tools an effective problem solver might use include Cause-and-effect analysis with an Ishikawa diagram, Value Stream Mapping, Pareto Charts and various types of metrics such as Control Charts, Histograms, etc. There is a whole world of literature, practitioners, coaches and communities out there that specialize in problem solving techniques. I recommend you make good use of it.

EXAMPLE ROUTINE

This routine is literally a copy of Mike Rother's coaching questions. For the original card, and many more resources on Toyota Kata that he's made available for free (awesome!), please refer to his website: http://www-personal.umich.edu/~mrother/Homepage.html

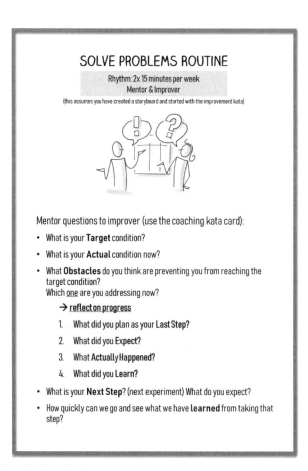

Figure 4.32 – Solve Problems Routine

Part V:

Getting started - Transforming your leadership system

Ready to get started with Obeya? Let's get into the more practical details of making it happen for your team. We'll look at the conditions for starting, what to look for in terms of facilities and the room, go through the transformation steps and look at some tips and pitfalls to help get your team started.

This chapter describes practical steps that should all be executed in order to support a successful Obeya transformation. If you have done just a few of these steps up until now, you could consider planning for the remaining ones to lock in aspects that will help make a success out of your Obeya endeavor.

It is called a transformation approach, and not an implementation plan, because participants will have to actually change the way they organize and look at their work. It goes beyond visualization but also dictates the way they have their meetings, their meeting schedule, the output of each meeting and how they are facilitated and coached.

The purpose of a transformation approach is simply to manage and communicate expectations. This plan should be agreed upon between at least the sponsor, the coach and the facilitator. Also, having some form of screening with one of the participants can be very valuable to check its practical feasibility and getting the first buy-in before presenting the plan to the rest of the leadership team.

The below overview provides a basic layout of a possible Transformation Approach.

Figure 5.1 – Example Obeya Transformation Approach steps

LEADING WITH OBEYA IS AS PRACTICAL FOR A LEADERSHIP TEAM AS SCRUM IS FOR DEVELOPMENT TEAMS

The great thing about Obeya is it provides a very practical structure of leadership activities. One could go as far as to say that a leadership team adopting Obeya is approaching the same transformation as an operational team that starts with Scrum. Where Scrum is a practical way to apply Agile principles for a team, Obeya offers a practical approach to applying Lean & Agile principles on a leadership level.

Similarity can be found in the aspects of adopting principles as a way of thinking and acting, implementing visual management with a Scrum board, agreeing on ceremonies like the daily Scrum, planning and review meetings, and, of course, to visualize the work and performance of the team.

One of the benefits of looking at the introduction of a new way of working in this way, is that there is structure. You won't have to debate the structure as it is a proven way of working. Having a systematic work method that is tested and proven on teams lowers the bar for acceptance. Having principles only and having to interpret them and transform them into sustainable behaviors without a practical way of working is incredibly hard and leads to variability and therefore potential waste.

How long is all of this going to take? Well that depends on your team and their willingness (eagerness & commitment) and ability (skills & knowledge) to work with Obeya. Some teams get to a level that's delivering benefits in a month or two, others might struggle for half a year before they finally start solving problems and gain real value out of working with Obeya. The trick is probably to want to make it work and get the value out of it. If you don't really want or need it to work, you'll struggle even with the smallest problems.

Step 1: Approach agreed

In this first step a senior leader together with a coach or someone from the team who will help get started designing the outline for the seven steps. The coach advises on common pitfalls and the following of the key aspects of the kick-starter steps to maximize the chance of a successful outcome. If the existing coach does not yet have experience with Obeya, it is useful to ask the help of a coach that does, so during the seven steps there is knowledge transfer as well.

SENIOR SPONSOR ON-BOARD

The senior sponsor should be driver for this transformation in the way of working. If that person doesn't want this, then you're likely to fail in achieving any improvements. Therefore, it's important to get the senior sponsor on-board by agreeing on the approach in this first step.

The senior sponsor must be able to motivate the team toward the goal or improvement they seek and infuse a sense of urgency (if any) to start this transformation. This motivation should be focused on achieving the actual desired state, rather than the rigorous and dogmatic implementation of a tool.

IDENTIFYING PARTICIPANTS: THE LEADERSHIP TEAM

Identifying the team members is part of defining the approach. Usually, the senior leader takes this responsibility in her role as team leader. The coach may advise on this, e.g. in terms of group size, level of involvement for each role, etc. Skills, knowledge and experience may be additional factors to look for in a leadership team.

When is it useful to bring people together as a team in an Obeya meeting? Here are a few ideas:
- When they strive for a common goal or purpose.
- When they have dependencies on one another.
- When they use the same resources (people, process technology).
- When they apply the same solution or use the same methods to come to a solution.

If there is no common will or purpose to work on an achievement together, don't use Obeya as a leadership instrument if people are not intending to work collaboratively to achieve a clearly defined common goal. After all, what would be left to lead?

EXPLORE FOCUS POINTS & KEY CHALLENGES

Each team is likely to be in a different phase in terms of development (forming, norming, storming, etc.) or capability knowledge, values and convictions, etc. They might be open to change or instead resist anything that affects their well ingrained routine that has existed for the past ten years. Every team is unique and that should be respected in a transformation approach. As such, they might have different challenges that could be addressed by tuning the kick-starter approach to this.

This is a good time to sit down with the team and assess whether they feel the need to change the way they currently work, whether they're motivated to make a success out of their Obeya journey. If not, then now is a an ideal time to address this before you move on to the next steps.

FINE-TUNE APPROACH TO TEAM MATURITY AND TIMING

The kick-start approach is a generic example of how one could start with an Obeya. It can be fine-tuned and timed according to the needs of the team. This is done by the coach and the senior sponsor. Usually, reflecting on the approach with at least one of the team members helps create buy-in and allows for the evaluation of feasibility.

This is a good time to assess the initial willingness and readiness of the team to start working with Obeya. If the team is ready and willing to learn, and if they feel there is a sense of urgency to get started, then you're on the right track.

OVERALL TIMELINES AGREED

The Obeya explanation should be scheduled as well as the overall desired timelines for completing the seven steps. The senior leader should be the driver for executing the steps within the times, the coach facilitates the pace.

Step 2: Obeya explained

This phase is all about having the team understand what they are about to commit to. Commitment is important because they are probably required to make changes on different aspects of how they are used to working, such as how they approach problems, when they have meetings, how these meetings take place, etc. Nothing comes automatically in the Obeya, the team will have to put hard and serious work and intellect into the process of creating and using an Obeya effectively. Before they start they must realize what this entails for them.

FAMILIARIZE THE TEAM WITH OBEYA

To learn about Obeya you should experiencing it first-hand. Go to an existing Obeya room inside your organization or do a reference visit at another organization. Standing with your team in an Obeya will engage all the senses of the team and is much more likely to help them understand what it is. Of course, someone should be present who can explain properly how the room works and how its users have developed it. The most powerful way of doing this is having your team observe another (experienced) team use the Obeya.

ESTABLISH A COMMON REFERENCE FOR SEEING, LEARNING AND ACTING

Obeya isn't about placing existing reports on the wall. Rather, the way we are able to define our system and expose problems is where the real challenge lies. But this is not a skill that comes naturally in management teams. Traditionally, problems are a bad thing and should be avoided. But now, we make a 180 degree turn and look to start exposing problems so we can improve. That turn is not to be underestimated.

It is imperative the team on a basic level is familiarized with the principles related to Obeya. Even though some may claim to be Lean or Agile experts, this does not automatically confer a shared frame of reference for how the leadership team should visualize their system in the Obeya.

One of the ways to do this is simply by doing a workshop or providing some degree of training with the whole team, preferably putting what has been learned into practice straight away in the actual Obeya. You can use the Reference Model from this book as a frame of reference.

EXPLAIN APPROACH TO EXPOSING & SOLVING PROBLEMS

Most managers will stick to shooting from the hip if they are not guided to adopt the improvement method and the philosophy behind it. What's the problem with that? Nothing, if you want to keep getting what you always got. Should you be looking for truly sustainable improvements for your team and their results, it is time to change the way you look at problems.

Having tools for improvement is one thing, but what's more important is to understand the underlying pattern of thinking. Everything that happens in the Obeya is intrinsically linked — the thought pattern of continuous improvement, setting a challenge, understanding the current condition, setting a target condition and moving towards it. It shows in the Lead Successful Strategies area (which sets a challenge), and then when we are building up our Drive Performance and Deliver Value areas that we are setting both current and target conditions towards that challenge. If we're not seeing the results we expect, we're using the Act & Respond and Solve Problems area to run experiments and activities that should help us achieve our goals.

This way of thinking must be introduced to the team through a presentation or (preferably) a workshop in which they try it out, to make very explicit how we'll be using Obeya, since we'll need to commit to it in the next phase. Fortunately, it is completely common sense, just like following the Plan Do Check Act cycle for improvement.

TYPICAL ROLES IN AND AROUND THE OBEYA

Though the Obeya is in principle an open room for everybody to visit, it is recommended to have a few roles defined for the direct stakeholders. To avoid confusion, clear ownership of information and agreement on what that means should be established right at the launch of any Obeya. Without it, people may start looking at each other for responsibilities or refuse ownership of information which in turn can lead to reduced levels of participation, messy meetings with outdated information, and so on.

So to have a few roles defined helps clarify responsibilities. Here are a few generic roles that help keep your Obeya organized. Do note that these are generic descriptions, a role is not limited to one person and is not a full-time job.

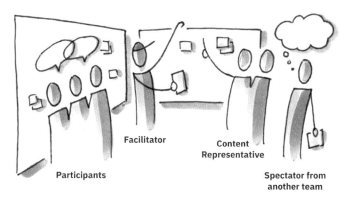

Figure 5.2 – Roles in and around the Obeya

SPONSOR

Generally a (or the most) senior manager that participates in the Obeya sessions and leads the setup and development of the Obeya way of working. The owner is the primary representative for the Obeya of her or his team on the next management level up, in case of a cascade. Also, the owner will work together with the facilitator or coach to improve everything in and around the workings of the Obeya. Ownership by this person is key to the success, therefore, things like a background in Lean, previous Obeya experience and sufficient powers of persuasion with her or his peers are useful characteristics for the person who takes on this role.

ACTIVE PARTICIPANT

Basically anybody (and any role) who actively works with the information on the walls by joining any one of the Obeya sessions. Participants should make sure they review the information on the walls ahead of the actual session to reduce reading time during the session. Participants who are part of the team that operates in the Obeya can each be improvers at the improvement wall with help of the coach.

PASSIVE PARTICIPANT/SPECTATOR

Often, the context that is created in an Obeya meeting can also be beneficial for members of the organization who are not directly involved in the leadership team that's having the meeting. So instead of actively participating they are observing the meeting so as not to disturb the process of the leaders, passively sharing in the context at the same time. Sometimes there are experts there at the request of a leader to briefly (think no more than five minutes) elaborate on a specific topic or on their learnings, for example, in relation to an improvement. They are asked for brief active participation on a specific subject.

CONTENT REPRESENTATIVE

The content on the walls is provided by an agreed content provider who is also a participant. The content owners are responsible for making information available on the walls on time before a session, or delegating this to anyone in their team. They are responsible for creating a selection of information that fits their responsibilities. Thoroughly knowing the contents of the presented information and create more in-depth knowledge of the workings of the related system by involvement in improvements (related) to the metric is also part of the content provider's job.

FACILITATOR

Anyone who helps on an operational level in the Obeya, either during or outside the sessions. The primary goal of the facilitator is to support the smooth planning and execution of Obeya sessions on a logistical level. This can be as simple as making sure there are enough pens and Post-Its as well as actively facilitating the sessions based on the routines. This role can be combined with the coach. Also, the team members themselves can pick up a rotating schedule to facilitate the sessions, if they manage to master the routines. When they do facilitate, it is still useful to have the occasional presence of a coach who will help avoid delay in running the routines, which is sure to present itself without the outside involvement of a coach.

The facilitator should be barely 'visible' but at the same time help the team follow the routine in the most effective way. A facilitator is the liaison between facilities management and the team, they also setup the room and any communications systems to prepare for the meetings.

COACH

This is the Obeya expert with a coaching background that helps the group and its individuals develop their leadership behavior according to their own ambitions, learn about the Obeya way of working, setup and challenge their content, etc. The main difference between the coach and the facilitator is that the coach has in-depth knowledge and experience on Obeya as well as team coaching and preferably personal coaching and is able to focus on achieving higher levels of maturity, whereas the facilitator's main focus is logistics as well as making sure sessions are run smoothly.

A good coach will guide you in your journey to define the right Strategic Capabilities, metrics, visuals, etc. But he or she will also help you get started in the right rhythm and routines for each wall. A very important success factor in implementing Obeya is the coach representing the team's 'external conscience', reflecting on their behavior when they deviate from their ambitions. Even the more experienced teams sometimes get sloppy in their routines which immediately puts the effectiveness of the Obeya at risk.

The coach can also facilitate, but depending on the characteristics of the team it may be quite a challenge to both coach on behavior as well as facilitate the routine of the meeting.

The coach and/or facilitator is sometimes referred to as Obeya Master, which is sort of a Scrum master for leadership teams on the level of facilitation and support for the team. In this book we will keep referring to the roles of coach and facilitator to be more specific in terms most people are familiar with.

Before starting with Obeya, there is usually a certain need for someone to explain to a leadership team what the way of working could mean to them and how it should be implemented. The coach or Obeya expert role is then taken with the distinct purpose on the advising of how things should be implemented, rather than responding to a coaching question and guiding a person or a team through the process of thought. Leading with Obeya as described in this book is mature enough for an experienced coach to introduce to a team effectively and train them up to a beginner level of understanding to get started on their journey.

STARTING WITH THE END IN MIND

The below table depicts a current (classical) leadership system, and a target condition in which Obeya is used as a tool within a Leadership System that operates effectively. Reviewing, editing and agreeing on a target condition with the team helps bring agreement on improvements towards that target condition. It also helps them understand the differences between how the leadership team works today and how it will work when we're using Obeya.

Obeya Challenge:

Enable collaborative learning and continuous improvement for all our teams so we can make optimal use of our scarce resources to deliver value for customers while fulfilling our purpose, addressing the needs of planet, people and profit.

Getting to the target condition isn't done overnight. It will take years if you'll even reach it at all. That's why we refer to using Obeya as a transformation, rather than an implementation. You can implement the use of walls and visuals on it, but you cannot implement changed and coherent behavior in and around your leadership team as if it were a washing machine.

TIP - Don't judge the book by its cover! The effectiveness of the Obeya does not come from the visible parts on the walls. Instead, what you see on the walls is the result of how the leadership team works, interacts and understands their leadership and production systems. So don't judge a book by its cover when you walk into any Obeya. You might walk into a room that looks really neat and impressive, but that says nothing about how it is used and whether the team can be effective in the room. Similarly, if it looks a tad messy it might be it is simply being used a lot which is a good sign.

	Current condition	Target condition
LEAD SUCCESFUL STRATEGIES	**Strategy** only exists as an overview document. Communication only takes place on, and from, senior management level. Teams carry out their work according to known patterns and the status quo.	Strategy is translated in every department from CEO level to operations through dialogue and feedback which creates understanding, buy-in and increases feasibility. Teams connect their daily activities and results to the purpose. They inspect, adapt & improve their way of working to meet the strategic objectives.
DRIVE PERFORMANCE	**Performance** is visible in output like budget burndown, sales, number of users etc. KPIs are set based on Management By Objective (MBO). There is focus only on results, and not the road towards the results or the system that is supposed to produce them.	Performance is linked to the strategy, so leaders can set clear priorities. Performance is visible on process level, like process cycle efficiency, lead time, specified and actual budget utilization, customer feedback, etc. The team aims to create insights on the system level of value creation and to make improvements.
DELIVER VALUE	**Value creation** process is unpredictable for teams or departments that are doing the work, each with their own targets. There is a list of number one priorities that are all picked up simultaneously, effectively delaying all of them. There are no insights in resource utilization in relation to the realization of strategic objectives.	Value creation (-chain) is visible as a process or a plan and as such has become more predictable. Bottlenecks are visualized and the flow of work is picked up one by one, using weighted priorities from the strategy.

ACT & RESPOND	Leaders are hard to reach for employees outside any one-on-one meetings they might have. **Problems and requests** are handled by email until the problem is big enough to give priority. Problems stay unaddressed or unsolved for a long period of time.	Leaders are several moments a week at a fixed location and time to address problems and requests from the teams in an early stage. In this way leaders can facilitate the teams in an optimal way to create value towards the strategy.
SOLVE PROBLEMS	Problems are solved **ad hoc**. Problems and root causes stay invisible because of troubleshooting and the reward of 'green' reports, where there is a disconnect between the results in the report and the reality perceived on the work floor.	Leaders are visibly **continuously improving** with their teams. Using scientific thinking and improvement Kata leaders will be in constant dialog with the team to realize practical problem solving that are in the way to achieve strategic objectives.
RHYTH & ROUTINE	**Meetings** are ad hoc and **chaotically planned** in agendas; Creating moments to align teams costs a lot of time, because of busy agendas. Meetings have to be planned far into the future, reducing the ability to respond to change. Meetings often **lack** a **clear goal and agenda,** people come unprepared. Objective fact based information to take decisions is lacking.	Almost all meetings are planned using a fixed rhythm and routine. As such the leadership team is available to respond to changes and problems, big or small. An agreed objective and agenda, where factual information is visible and accessible for the team so decisions can be made. Meetings are considered effective, leaders have more time for their teams and there is more space in the agenda to be present on the floor (Gemba walks) or for specific meeting subjects.

Table 5.1 — Moving from current to target condition in the Obeya

Step 3: Commit

Now that our team understands what we're getting ourselves into, it's time to capitalize on that commitment through some explicit agreements.

AGREEMENT: GO AND TAKE THE REMAINING STEPS

At this point, the senior leader of our team might ask for an agreement from each of our team members to start committing to participation in the remaining steps and adopting the Obeya way of working from then onwards.

The remaining steps require an investment to some degree from the leadership team members. We must gather information from various sources, think about goals, targets, possible thresholds, etc. At least another two days lay ahead in which we are expected to dedicate our time to filling the Obeya walls. In other words, we'll need to start clearing our agendas. Fortunately, by now, we'll know why and, to some degree what, to expect.

AGREEMENT ON COACHING & FACILITATION

People are intrinsically not very good at reflection, and we are easily tricked into drawing false or biased conclusions (Kahneman, 2011).[69] Moreover, we overestimate ourselves more often than we do others. Given that it's inherent to being human, this is something we have to deal with. It starts with acknowledging the fact that it would be good to have an unbiased third person that will give us honest objective observations and reflection on progress towards our way of working and our common goals.

For that reason a coach is not just a good idea, but more likely a requirement, especially at this stage, and that's regardless of the maturity of our team. In fact, more mature teams often ask for more coaching as they become more aware of their own tendency to bias as well as a better understanding of how much we don't know we don't know.

In asking a coach to support the team consider the following:
- The team members must agree to be coached as a group and individuals.
- The coach should have a license to operate (preferably a written statement

describing the intentions, goals and approach for coaching).
- The coach should be well versed in Lean & Agile ways of working and be competent with Obeya. Also, a coach should have training & experience as a coach, preferably in both individual and team coaching.

RHYTHM AND ROUTINE AGREED

Now that the team understands why certain things are done in a specific way, for example by following a structured routine that asks questions so we can avoid bias in meetings, it is time to start talking about how to make it happen.

At this point, explaining the recommended rhythm and routine will help the team translate the next steps in the kick-starter approach to their daily practice. Also, it will provide them with the looking glass to start the refinements. They'll know what they'll be looking for in the Obeya meetings so they can start collecting data and visualizing it in such a way that it will help them understand the production and leadership systems as well as spot any problems.

Starting with the actual new rhythm and routine can be a daunting task, as most people will have to move around meetings in their schedules. At first, the struggle to get this done will likely expose a problem: the absence of having a rhythm leads to a random mess of meetings which makes it hard to find time for effective alignment.

If you want to tackle any discussions that might be sparked about whether to spend more time on meetings because of the Obeya, then now is a good time to do a brief analysis of the actual meetings our team members have and which ones will be replaced by the Obeya as well as which ones will become obsolete.

Since it will take a while to get all the meetings in each team member's agenda, it's wise to plan a few weeks ahead, before the actual rhythm and first Obeya meeting starts.

SIGNING A CHARTER TO CONFIRM THE COMMITMENTS MADE

To be sure what the team is committing to and to keep one step ahead of ambiguous decision making, it is a good practice to sign a charter with the team; physically have the team members sign it and put it visibly in the Obeya. This will help the team members and the coach point out any deviations on the path to their commitment. The charter should include the goal of working with Obeya and the coaching license to operate. It can also contain the team values which are useful for coaching behavior.

> **TIP** - Signing a charter with your team in which they read and physically sign their commitment to making this a success helps them keep that commitment later on. They can refer to it while coaching each other or a coach can use it as a license to operate.

ARE YOU READY, WILLING AND ABLE?

Ready – should we do it and do it now?

When is a good time to start to improve the way you lead your organization? Well it helps if the team has space in their heads for System II thinking.

It may be easiest to start at a moment when the team faces a fresh start of some kind — after the Summer or at the start of a new year, particularly when there is a strategic review or planning session scheduled. I personally always consider the cost of delay. It always sounds a bit silly to me when teams claim to be working too hard on a deadline to improve their ability to meet that deadline with Obeya, but it is completely conceivable from a System I type of thinking.

Starting your Obeya with a Lean or Agile transformation is always a good idea, after all the transformation should be aimed at improving the Organizational Capabilities in order to achieve our purpose. And what better place to do that than in an Obeya?

Obeya has, in principle, no restrictions in terms of implementation in any kind of organization, no matter your industry or size. If your organization has no experience with Lean, Agile, Obeya can still be a useful instrument on one condition: you must be willing to adopt the way of working and the underlaying principles and make them your own.

Finally, being ready also means that you know why you want to start with Obeya. Why Obeya? What expectations do you have, what problems that you're currently experiencing would you like to solve? If you don't have an answer to these questions then perhaps now is not a good time to start.

> *"I don't think every team will be able to benefit from using an Obeya. If a team is not working well together, an Obeya won't change this. There has to be a strong buy-in of teams using it and the leader of the team must understand it, want it and go for it as well, otherwise it will be difficult to get the real value out of it. The most successful teams using an Obeya have are strong believe in the concept, designed an initial Obeya based on their own needs and never stop developing their Obeya based on a rhythm for short cycle improvements."*

– Leendert Kalfsbeek, IT Manager

Willing – what are we going to give up to do this?

Without a desire to change, a sense of urgency or a real need or willingness to improve, any change is going to be very difficult. An Obeya transformation is not about whether the tool fits the team's current way of working, it's about whether the team is willing to change and improve their way of working.

There is a pretty big difference between using a wall to create a life-size Gantt chart (the same one you already had in your project planning tool), and setting up an Obeya. The Obeya works as a system with the areas and the principles as its parts. If you start leaving parts of it out, you'll find it seriously affects the outcome of the system. If you plan on cherry picking the Obeya elements and not including vital parts like the Rhythm & Routine or Continuously Improve principle, then you risk creating a room that delivers the exact behavior and results as you have been getting in the past.

If you plan to embark on a Lean or Agile transformation, the Obeya can be a very powerful catalyst for this transformation, supporting management teams in going through the change of the transformation while keeping them aligned with what's happening with the operational teams. Whereas some Lean and Agile leadership philosophies and training can be somewhat intangible to apply in the workplace, the Obeya is a platform for leaders to bring Lean and Agile leadership into their daily practice. They won't even have to call it Lean or Agile.

Obeya helps teams adopt Lean and Agile principles through practical routines, introducing habits and ways of thinking, supported by visual management. When adopting a different way of working like this you cannot think your way into it; you have to start doing it. That's the power of using a (more or less prescriptive) approach like Obeya as described in this book.

Able – do we have the right skills to get this working?

In terms of ability, let's assume that if you are in a leadership position, you possess the intellectual capability to work with Obeya, especially since it is all very much common sense.

But the team should be open to the fact that they'll be learning new skills or using their existing skills differently. Here are some skills needed from the team, and we should check if they are sufficiently represented. If not, we should address them through training or temporary hiring of competencies during the transformation approach so we can make them our own.

Skills & Knowledge	Team members	Coach
Business Administration & statistics	X	X
Leadership	X	X
Scientific thinking	X	X
Coaching	X	X
Improvement method (Toyota Kata)	X	X
Product / Service knowledge	X	
Market & Domain knowledge	X	
Applied knowledge of methodology (e.g. Lean or Agile)	X	X
Expert knowledge on methodology		X
Expert knowledge on Obeya		X

Table 5.2 – Who should have certain Skills & Knowledge

This book aims to provide a starting point for transforming your current management habits to a more effective way of working with Obeya, achieving higher levels of effectiveness with your team. The basic standard provided can be adopted as a starting point for your improvement journey. You should always keep in mind that this journey will never end. The journey really is the destination in this case.

Keep an open mind towards feedback and focus on the learning capability. Then use this capability to also improve the way you use Obeya. Just don't forget to make sure you first master the basics of the Obeya before you make any serious changes, otherwise you might lose the system all together.

WHAT WORKING WITH OBEYA AND CREATING TRANSPARENCY MIGHT DO WITH BEHAVIOR

Since the Obeya can be a radical change from the current way of working, it introduces certain aspects in the way of working that some might resist more heavily than others. Examples of resistance you might encounter:

- **Transparency on how you work**

  Team members might feel uncomfortably exposed or controlled when being transparent about their results and how they achieve them. They might feel that with others looking at what they are doing, they are giving up autonomy over their way of working. Others might be judgmental, trying to intervene with how they do their job.

- **Transparency on results**

  If trust is low, team members might think senior leaders are seeking to find data that will provide the basis for the next round of reducing FTEs. If there is little or no trust in the organization, the latter fear is probably justified. Hence, a new problem is exposed. If this is the case, making very explicit agreements with senior leadership on what you are about to do to create safety for the team members is a likely prerequisite to get the team on board. In the Obeya, the emphasis must be on the learning, not the results.

- **Accountability**

  Taking accountability takes courage, especially in an organization where people lack the authority to make decisions over an autonomous product or services and do not want to be punished for the errors of others. If people are reluctant to take accountability there might be problems such as (1) fear (you get punished if things go wrong instead of focusing on the learning aspect of problems), or (2) a problem with autonomy — if you do not have the authority to make decisions over a certain product or services but you are still expected to be accountable for it. This might expose a bigger problem. If you find you lack authority to make meaningful decisions in your Obeya, perhaps it's time to talk about how your organization is organized.

Step 4: Set the stage

Ready to prepare your Obeya? It should be accessible for the team and they should be able to use the facilities (lines, stickies, pens, etc.).

FINDING A SUITABLE LOCATION

At this point, if you haven't found a suitable location, then this is a good time to do so. A few tips for assessing whether a location is suitable:

- Accessible for both the team and relevant members of the organization;
- Lots of space, preferably on a (magnetic) white wall or two;
- Allowed to place content on the walls;
- The location should always be available for the team to have their sessions;
- The location should be accessible for non-team members to gather information or context.

It helps other people to understand what they're looking at if you place a sign with the name of your team and the Obeya, perhaps including the rhythm for each session during the week.

ROOM AND FACILITIES

So you've got yourself a room, or a wall, or a sizeable whiteboard. Great! Now what? First of all it's good to think about how you intend to use the Obeya. Do you intend to do a lot of drawing and sketching? Then whiteboards, perhaps glass walls are your thing. Do you intend to put a lot of paper on the wall? Then magnetic walls are probably useful. Or, if all of the above is just not possible you could consider using a re-stick glue stick which magically turns every piece of paper into a reusable sticky note.

Maximize wall space

The ideal wall in an Obeya has magnetic whiteboard covering from floor to ceiling. The benefit of these types of walls is you can use them both for writing and for sticking paper on them using magnets. In fact, there are a lot of practical magnets in all kinds of shapes that will help strengthen the visuals. Since the walls are fully magnetic you can stick these magnets anywhere you like without having to use tape or blu-tack.

If possible, avoid walls that have a lot of windows unless you intend to use them. It's often hard to read paper that's stuck on a window. Also, I once encountered a team that was worried that people in the building next to them could actually read the company-specific strategic information they were using on the walls (if those people in the next building decided to bring binoculars).

TIP - Talk to your facility management team early! On one occasion the facility management team had done their homework by looking up Obeya online and then created a really nice looking room with fancy looking glass plates in front of the magnetic boards. Unfortunately they hadn't asked us how we intended to use that room and instead of writing on the walls (in which case glass covered white walls are really nice), we would hardly be doing any writing at all. Rather, we intended to use hundreds of small magnets to place small milestone papers for a big portfolio wall. In the end, the facility management team took down the fancy glass off the walls and increased the size of the magnetic walls. We ended up with really good facilities in that Obeya, but not before some time, material and money were wasted.

Mobile whiteboards

Make sure there is plenty of room to walk around. Being able to use a mobile white-board (preferably foldable so you can maximize usable surface) helps with mobility and positioning areas just where you want them. The fact that it's mobile enables you to move it around the room depending on where space should be created for the team to walk around and interact with the visuals.

I've seen operational teams ride their own mobile whiteboards into the Obeya for their meetings with the leadership team.

Create an open space, take care of sensitive information

The basic assumption is this space is accessible to everybody who is allowed to walk the office building freely. Some management teams have chosen to limit access to their Obeya. Depending on what part of the organization is represented in the Obeya, there may be a higher level of classified or sensitive information. This can cause teams to decide their Obeya should be locked up from outsiders.

Openness and transparency at every level is crucial for creating a culture in which everybody is involved and working on the same purpose. However, there are teams that feel they need to lock their room to protect information that, in fact, cannot be shared with other members of the same organization. Usually, the actual sensitive information is no more than 5% of the information available in their Obeya. Exceptions are, of course, teams that per definition operate in a work environment that deals with classified information, highly sensitive information, or with information that has high strategic (market) value in itself. Even in those cases, teams should reconsider.

What's most important, though, is management should be able to discuss all topics they need to without feeling they can't speak openly because topics are sensitive. For example, when it comes to discussing plans that may affect employees' jobs, they might prefer to have a private session, in which case, being able to close a door could be preferable. I've seen teams hold open sessions where interested stakeholders (staff, senior management or operational team members) are allowed to observe.

Perhaps the best group I've witnessed was at ING Bank. They actually had an audience from time to time, and had to limit the number of spectators because the interest from other parts of the organization was so high. They truly set inspiring standards both in terms of showing how effective these meetings can be, as well as their openness. How many management team meetings have you ever attended because they were both interesting and open to colleagues?

Materials

To make an Obeya visually attractive for the team, you'll need materials that help transform ordinary paper into an Obeya wall that supports cognitive ease for its users. You'll need facilities that help create visual outlines in the room, like lines and frames. Make sure you have enough facilities and materials for the launch of the Obeya; it might take some time getting everything you need delivered to the room.

What kind of materials do you need to be able to put your prints on the wall and display them in a neat and attractive way? First of all, there is the printer. Because you'll be working with signaling functions and, therefore, probably color, you might want to use a color printer.

Materials you'll need even if you don't have magnetic white walls:
- Separator lines (usually 3mm wide tape that is also used for lineage on paint jobs).
- Sticky notes and pens.
- Restick glue stick (can turn any piece of paper into a sticky note! Very useful if you don't have magnetic walls).
- Whiteboard and/or permanent markers, preferably in a variety of colors.

If your Obeya walls are made out of magnetic materials then you can also add magnetic items to your materials list:
- Magnets in the shape of smileys and warning signs.
- Magnetic frames (A3 or A4) to contain e.g. metrics and use a red or green signal color.
- Lots of small magnets (preferably matching the color of your wall so they don't stand out) to put papers on the wall.

GOING DIGITAL OR NOT

Should you apply digital means in your Obeya? Believe it or not, there is such a thing as technology bias, where we tend to believe things are better on a screen. Let's start by remembering that in the Obeya, everything is about the quality of the interaction of the people, which is always done best face to face, there is simply no replacement. Consider the difference in your perceived engagement between watching an online training video or having the actual trainer in the room with you.

However, digital means are very useful in the Obeya in the following applications:
- Single source of truth like an intranet page where all the reports in the Obeya can also be found when you can't be in the actual room.
- An information system like a portfolio management system that easily filters through information to deep-dive for certain questions, finding links and statuses beyond a level of detail that can be displayed in the Obeya.
- Means for audio/video calls with the group (make sure video is pointed at the people so they can read the non-verbal communication).

Again, being together in one room is always better. Also, working with physical paper greatly enhances your relationship with the data and will leave stronger impressions as more parts of the brain are engaged (e.g. motion, touch, etc.).

Let's end with a few common misconceptions:
- Writing an action digitally is faster than on a sticky note (the latter is much faster).
- If people don't write clearly on a sticky note their actions will be much better documented when they enter it into a digital system (it will be just as cryptic as before).
- If people do not have the discipline to update their information on physical paper before a session, then they won't magically get that discipline when working on a digital system.
- For all systems: garbage in is garbage out. If your tool is great but it's loaded with wrong or biased information it is useless.

INFORMATION VS COMMUNICATION

Is having a portfolio wall the same as looking in your portfolio management tool? It's not; the portfolio wall is an immersive means or communication and provides overview. The portfolio management tool is an information system that's great for digging into the details. For this point, remember, both can be used next to each other but they fulfill different functions.

One thing is for sure, if you're in the Obeya to learn, you're best off with the freedom to create overviews that have the flexibility to fully support that learning. You don't want to be constricted to the format and display functionality of a digital system.

GATHER DATA

While some are working on the physical aspects of the room, the leadership team members are gathering data in preparation for the initial refinement session. What they should be looking for: Strategic documents that help define the purpose fill the 'Lead Successful Strategies 'area as well as portfolio information of how they Deliver Value and reports that show how they Drive Performance.

TRAINING YOUR COACH

This is a good time to start training your coach if your designated coach is not experienced in Obeya. Try to do a training and get the designated coach up to speed so he or she can facilitate the Obeya sessions from day one and build up their capabilities to a basic level during the first ten weeks of using Obeya.

Step 5: Refine the information

PREPARE TO SETUP THE AREAS

When we refine the information that your team works with, we'll immediately start building the actual Obeya. The sooner things become tangible on the wall, the better. Below is an example of the order in which areas are being setup in the Obeya. This is not necessarily a linear process.

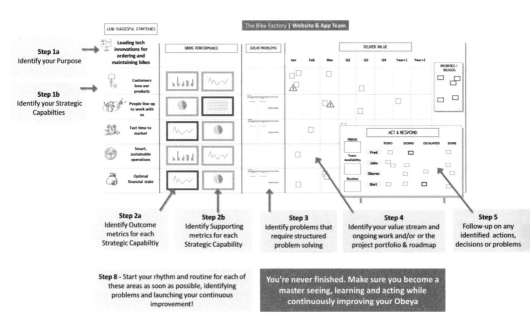

Figure 5.3 - Overview of steps to setup your Obeya areas

LEAD SUCCESSFUL STRATEGIES

In this stage the team will take the first steps for transforming the current strategy into the start of what will be the Lead Successful Strategies area. Also, we should be able to define the Strategic Capabilities we'll need to Drive Performance as well as define the products, services and key projects & programs in Deliver Value area, on a level of granularity that is relevant for our team at this time.

This is often uncharted or neglected territory where our team will have to put in serious intellectual effort. Taking your time for this is a prerequisite, don't try to squeeze this into a 60 minute pressure cooker, rather timebox it for half a day.

INITIAL FILLING OF CONTENT FOR DELIVER VALUE & DRIVE PERFORMANCE

Now that the team has created an outline of what matters, they can use that to filter through the available data they gathered. As such, an immediate filtering of data that is reported but, perhaps, not (that) relevant will be exposed and can be disregarded. The team will use the relevant reports and also find out whether they are missing any relevant information. This is the first step in filling the walls and exposing problems. This will easily take another day to make a good start (you won't be able to finish).

START WITH A SMALL SELECTION OF VISUALS

The good thing about starting with a small selection of visuals is that any report that is not available will be summoned on demand, following the Lean principle of pull. If there is a demand for it, then it will likely be used. In doing so, the expected effect should be that for each of the Strategic Capabilities there will be at least one report. And if there is a desire for the team to drill down into the details of a report in order to increase actionability and accountability, then that can be a good next step if it relates to a priority challenge. Of course, any newly introduced report should be carefully reviewed over its first weeks of introduction to make sure it adapts into a stable, valuable report that the team can use effectively.

If an Obeya is plastered with reports, and information appears outdated, it's probably time to start tearing a few papers off the wall. Having too many reports is both administrative overburden as well as visually disrupting the cognitive process for team members who might get distracted or waste time debating why a report hasn't been updated.

Step 6: Starting the routines

ADOPTING THE RHYTHM AND ROUTINE

Adopting a rhythm and routine for each area in the Obeya will be a pretty big change in the schedule of a manager. Initially, it might seem that there's a lot of extra meetings involved. However, what must be stressed from the start is that this *is* the work that we're planning, rather than something extra. It's a replacement, not an addition to your existing schedule. And, if setup properly, the manager should be able to fulfill all of her management tasks within the scheduled routines while freeing up time and mind space to facilitate and coach her teams. In essence, managers should be able to do more in a similar amount of time, thus, spending their time more effectively.

> *"One of the team members was against adopting the Obeya meetings immediately when we made the suggestion. But once we explained which meetings he could actually stop doing because we would be replacing them with Obeya meetings, he was all in."*
>
> **– Sytze Hiemstra, Tribe Lead**

Once you do have the meetings scheduled, the format of doing a routine is likely to be significantly different from how you did your meetings before. In many classical ways of meeting, there is an agenda (or not) prepared by the chairman or facilitator which prioritizes topics based on whatever is discussed as most urgent at that time by the chairman, often influenced by other members of the leadership team. During the meeting everybody leans back while the chairman follows the fixed agenda and waits until it's their turn to either share their opinion or provide relevant information towards a topic. What tends to happen is that you're in a 1.5 hour meeting with only one topic that was relevant to you, which was so low on the agenda that it got pushed out of the time slot by lengthy, sometimes heated discussions on topics that were scheduled earlier. There goes your precious time.

"The Obeya helped bringing more focus into the conver-sations of the leadership team. What are the things we have to talk about and what should we talk about first? This is the first observation you can see with teams start-ing with Obeya."

– Sven Dill, Agile Coach

Obeya meetings are much more focused meetings that, because of the systems thinking & accountability principle, should provide relevancy for most of the team members. Moreover, it prioritizes problems for discussion based on their impact & urgency right at the start of the meeting, rather than following an agenda set by whomever manages to influence the person controlling the agenda. Perhaps, most importantly, meetings in the Obeya are not for lengthy debates and opinions, but to come to action and accountability as fast as possible based on available facts. If you want to talk content, don't spend more than five minutes of it with the pur-pose of creating just enough context for everybody to understand the problem, its context and to agree to the most valuable course of action. If there is more need to talk about the content to come up with the right actions, then this is usually only relevant for two or three people in the team, hence their action will be to schedule a follow-up discussion.

> **TIP** - A useful way of checking if your rhythm and routine is fit for the purpose is by asking the leadership team the following question: "Do you agree that all problems that needed to be addressed were addressed on time and have led to meaningful action?" If the answer is "no," then you might be uncovering room for improvement, either in your rhythm (being available to address problems faster) or routine (addressing them differ-ently, or finding faster ways to come to actions).

When adopting the rhythm and routines, make sure you pay attention to the ses-sions of teams that are related to your team. For example, make sure the operational teams can first have their stand-up so after it they can take the problems that need your support straight to your leadership stand-up in the Obeya. This creates a flow between the meetings that supports speed and effectiveness in tackling problems. It might look something like the below example schedule.

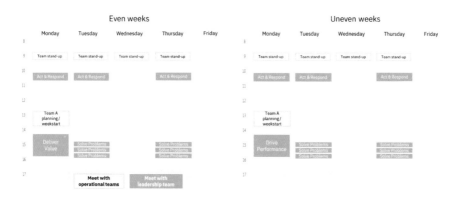

Figure 5.4 – Example agenda that includes participation on two team levels

Going straight into the routines

After the initial refinement is done, the room is basically ready for use. It is important to keep momentum, so try to roll straight into the routines that were agreed upon in step three by next week.

Also, the team should realize that the first few times of doing the routines might not go as smoothly as they expect. Following a routine is really quite different from the free-format management team meetings we've been having over the last decades. As we've learned in this book, the idea of adopting a routine is that you get good at it the more you practice. And it's the practice that we're after: learning & improving.

If you can, start all the routines and get rid of all the old meetings simultaneously. The longer these co-exist the less you will be able to gain real value from it in terms of winning time and effectiveness in meetings. The coach and the leadership team can sit together drawing up all the existing meetings and how and when to replace them with the new routines.

TIP - Do you know Shu Ha Ri? (The details are explained on the next page.) Don't change the routines in the first period unless it is absolutely necessary. There is a reason the routines are set up this way and we must first learn why before we should change them. This is part of developing your skills. The initial routines are your current best known way of doing things. Improve them, don't ditch them.

Additional coaching support

If you do not yet have an experienced coach available to your team directly, try to get an experienced coach to shadow coach the sessions in the background. The shadow coach should remain in the background and discuss observations with the designated coach for the team.

Do a retrospective

Scheduling the first retrospective right from the start and as part of the kick-start approach can be beneficial on several levels:
- The team knows when they'll evaluate the way of working so they'll be able to hold out until that session. In the meantime they can park their item on the board.
- You're sure it will happen and is not delayed due to late planning.
- Having a cadence for retrospectives can be useful so team members can save up their improvements for a specific moment. This avoids discussions on the method every session.

See if you can do a retrospective after about ten weeks of running the actual routines. This should give the team enough time to learn to do the routine up to a basic competency level and experience the benefits as well as learn about whether to change the routine, or the way they have used the routine.

Make sure you do the retrospective in such a way that improvements are implemented on the spot. Don't rush it by scheduling thirty extra minutes on top of a normal meeting, shooting improvements on stickies. It suggests a low priority for implementing improvements and the actions might not get done within due time. Your leadership team's time is too precious to waste on thinking of improvements that do not get implemented!

There is no shame in taking about 1.5 hours for the first retrospective. Usually, in this first meeting the fire-from-the-hip troubleshooter type manager reigns in shooting solutions at problems into the group, making it a session about emotions and subjectivity and who wins at having the best idea for a solution, largely run by a smaller portion of the team members. As such, good preparation of the retro is important:

- Use a timeboxed agenda.
- Start with why you're doing Obeya and what the target condition is to make sure improvements are focused on what is *needed* (not necessarily on what some of the participants might *want*).
- Make sure the improvement mindset is used to solve problems. Avoid ambiguous or biased statements like "the meeting takes too long," or "we are not as effective as we used to be." Tackle those complaints by putting them in the perspective of the challenge & target condition, and check the factual data. For example, if you have done so in step three, check the old schedule of the leadership to see how much time was needed.
- Make sure there is enough time to implement improvements during the session (e.g. a timeslot change on the rhythm, or a change in the routine). Improvements that cannot be implemented should be tagged to someone as action holder with a due date.

APPRECIATE YOUR LEARNING PATH - FIRST GET THE BASICS RIGHT

Perhaps the most important thing to keep in mind with Obeya is that you cannot cherry-pick, and you must learn to understand how things work together before you change anything, or else you'll be leading the system into ruin. In Lean, there is something called Shu Ha Ri that refers to the levels of understanding that people go through when learning new ways of working:

What (Shu) –

Understanding <u>what</u> you need to do. It starts with trusting the standard way of working and following the standard without (unintentional) deviations. The objective is to make the standard automatic so that it may be followed correctly and, of course, efficiently. Focus on trusting and following the standard in this phase, do not change the standard.

How (Ha) –

Understanding <u>how</u> the standard works within the system. What are its effects on the outcome of the goals we're trying to achieve? We start to see the value of the standard that we're using, and we can follow it almost blindly. Make small improvements in this phase if you see them, but only if you're sure you're not breaking other parts of the system.

Why (Ri) –

Understanding the <u>why</u>. We've moved beyond seeing the effects to understanding why we do things the way we do. We understand how the system operates with all its elements within and outside of its context. The standard is followed. At this point, we can initiate and coach more impactful improvements while being conscious of their effects on people, processes, the organization and the entire value chain.

"What I see a lot is that people want to use Obeya because it's hot and happening. Just like it happened with Scrum, Agile and the Spotify way of working. It's like a new trend and people feel they should follow it in order to show they are on top of market developments. I think more teams should think about what they want to achieve first and based on that, think about a suitable tool or approach. Each tool has a different recipe and impact on a team's dynamics. Choosing the wrong tool to solve a problem, could negatively impact the team's performance."

– Leendert Kalfsbeek, IT Manager

QUALITIES OF A GOOD MEETING

A good meeting should include:
- Clear responsibilities in the group and what their role and participation is in terms of decision making.

- Participants are willing and able to share their knowledge, experiences and viewpoints, but are also willing to receive them from others.
- There is up front clarity on whether the meeting should be convergent (e.g. making decisions, or picking the right solution) or divergent (e.g. generating ideas, or doing solution exploration).
- Part of a plan-do-check-act cycle: which Part Is the meeting for? Or are we doing the whole cycle in one meeting?

Step 7: Continuous improvement

Keep it going!

You've done it! You managed to survive the first period of using Obeya. Enough for the wax on, wax off, it's time you stood on your own feet to see if you mastered the moves of continuous improvement.

Keep in mind, there is no such thing as done in the Obeya, after all, we're continuously improving! Also there are no capability maturity levels you should strive for. The journey of continuous improvement will take you where you must go and it never ends. The good news: you entered a journey of getting (even) better at achieving your purpose for your professional life!

Coaching and facilitation

TRANSFORMING THE WAY YOU HAVE MEETINGS

There is potentially a lot of waste in traditional types of meetings and they have a negative impact on ourselves and our organization (Lencioni, 2004).[*] Moreover, satisfaction rates are low and they're just not a lot of fun.

---

[*]   Lencioni, 2004, *Death by Meeting*

In the Obeya, participants are standing (not seated) to keep them active, and topics are raised based on priority in terms of value rather than how important individual members rank them. Let's look at a few differences that await when transforming your meetings into Obeya meetings.

Traditional meetings	Obeya meetings
Focus on content and decision-making with the group	Focus on process and actions for decisionmakers (who can then make decisions)
Discussions prioritized by what the chairman thinks is most important	Discussions prioritized by what has the most impact on value for the customer (so problems first)
Actions defined are revisited during the next meeting	Actions defined are frequently monitored in stand-ups so they don't fall off the radar
Reports or PowerPoints are sent before (or during) the meeting	Visuals are always present in the room
Some meetings scheduled ad hoc, some on a regular base, but almost none finish on time	All but content meetings between content owners are pre-scheduled and finish on time.

Table 5.3 – Traditional vs Obeya meetings

PREPARE FOR MEETINGS

Once you start an Obeya meeting, you'll want to have as much value-add time as possible in terms of interaction and decision-making with team members. That means participants come prepared. They are aware of the updated information in the room, have informed themselves on the latest contextual developments and have sorted through the issues they want to address.

One of the most ineffective things to do in an Obeya meeting is to start reading the visuals for the first time during the meeting. It immediately introduces waiting time for the participants that did come prepared and might raise ill-prepared questions or assumptions from the hip to compensate for the lack of preparation (and the conviction that managers should have all the answers). Also if managers do prepare, they can ready their questions, do background checks if they see anything out of place. That in turn avoids having a discussion about the legitimacy of the visuals on the wall.

The value adding of the meeting does not come from being in the same room reading, but rather having a conversation sharing context, identifying problems and agreeing on actions and decisions to address these problems

The strongest experiences to create meaning and memory in our brain are done when a person in the Obeya explains to other people the development of a situation, while physically moving information about a piece of work from one place to another. The placement of the visualization is supported by visual guidelines (e.g. a timeframe from July to September), with a text explaining the context of the piece of work, perhaps supported by an icon or drawing to emphasize its meaning.

Figure 5.5 – Multi-activation in Obeya sessions using motion, pointing and talking to place emphasis

MAKING DECISIONS

Making quality decisions is not as easy as it may seem. There are often many interpretations and assumptions that come with decisions, especially if you were not previously part of the discussion. Sometimes, the discussion can be so heated that the quality of the decision suffers because everybody wants to move on to the next topic before any real decision has been made. It is up to the facilitator to help the team make quality decisions.

Here is how Facilitators help make sure quality decisions are made in the meeting:
- Using facts, not opinions or assumptions are used to come to the decision.
- Responding to the visuals and information that can be observed *in* the Obeya, not supposed facts that we cannot verify at the moment of making the decision. If we make a decision on a certain type of information, then we need it in our room (to be able to make good decisions).
- In case of an actionable agreement, the action holder (who) is defined, as well as the definition of done (the state to be achieved when the action is completed).
- A check is done on whether support is needed from the team or elsewhere to be able to put the decision into practice.

Avoid false consensus bias

Have you ever been in a meeting where the minutes of the last meeting were discussed and someone claims "that's not what we agreed upon"? Suddenly, everybody looks up and recalls their interpretation of what was agreed. Often, at least one or two of the group have a different recollection of what was agreed upon. This is the result of an ambiguous agreement.

What a team with help from its facilitator can do to avoid false consensus bias is to flag every decision by writing it down in a full sentence on a blue and wide sticky note and then putting it on the wall. This should preferably be done at the end of the discussion and the decision should be read out loud so there is no misunderstanding on what was decided. Once the agreement is made it can be put on the Agreements section of the Action Board, or any other visible place in the Obeya that the team agrees on.

Compliance and decision-making

A few years ago, I facilitated in an Obeya where the team was required to keep an audit trail of decisions for compliancy reasons. The team asked how to deal with this since we were now capturing the decisions made by the leadership team on blue stickies on a whiteboard instead of using an audit trail by email. After discussing the options with a compliance officer, we found a simple solution. For those decisions that were of the highest classification (e.g. impacting customers, leading to significant investments or causing media attention) we could simply share them via email with the team, either by taking a picture of the decisions or typing them in the email itself. This simple act would suffice as an audit trail. Moreover, the team found that only a fraction of their decisions would be of the kind that required an audit trail, which saved them a lot of effort trying to formally log every decision they made.

By looking into the policy of a decision on a sticky note, not only did the team discover that a lot was possible using just sticky notes instead of formal logging, but also the clarification of the policy lead to less burden on their administration.

WANT TO BE A TOP PERFORMER? GET A COACH

Having a coach does not mean you're not capable of doing your job. But not having a coach means you're limiting yourself to grow only as fast as you have access to your System 2. If you're a top performer in your organization, you're likely to use most of your System 2 on fighting fires and getting things done, while personal reflection is being pushed away by the daily buzz. Every sports team has a coach. It's easier to see flaws in others than in yourself, moreover, we're not always aware of our behavior versus how we intend to behave. Sometimes we intend to break old habits, and we could use a gentle (or strong) reminder if we don't. Maybe we need to become aware of habits we didn't even know we had.

Not all people are naturally favorable to coaching. Reasons expressed can be "what could I possibly learn from this person?" "I'm too busy for coaching," or "I work best alone." Let's take a step back and assume the human ego in the traditional management style has been developed in such a way that the person believes it must have all the answers as a manager. Since learning is part of our work instead of an extra, we should let go of the belief that we must know it all and institutionalize a coaching routine that not only helps us become better managers, but also helps us become coaches ourselves so we can in turn coach members in our teams.

An effective leader that helps people around them should do what any good coach does: ask questions that guide the athlete through the learning process, becoming aware of behavior and finding a path towards his own learning goals. At the same time an effective leader encourages the mentee to apply new ways of looking at problems so they learn to avoid bias and start working on problems structurally. In this way they become more creative and skilled problem solvers, and effectively become able to transfer this skill to others in your organization.

Coaching the team in the Obeya is effectively pretty straightforward, if you've got the routines and improvement mindset ingrained in your system (after a few years of practice) you're already well on your way to being an effective coach in the Obeya. Having knowledge and experience in personal- and team coaching is a big plus.

If you haven't got these skills in your organization, then having an external coach will help you get started. But the target condition must be that coaching is a skill and a capability that is developed inside the organization. You could start with an internal group of dedicated coaches to help you along, but remember the coaching skill should be part of the leadership skillset so you can scale.

Coaching and facilitating a leadership team can be a daunting challenge, especially with fast, verbal thinkers and alpha type leaders.[*] It is important to keep reflecting on (team) behavior and to help the team through the routine effectively.

It easily takes five years to become truly competent in coaching. Toyota has been using this model for a long time, grooming management and coaching capabilities from the inside rather than attracting managers from the outside (Rother, 2009). They might just have the biggest coaching capable leadership team in the world.

Virtual Obeya and remote collaboration

As we've learned, the Obeya should be set up and used in such a way that it supports our brains in effective decision-making. Our brain and our interaction with both content and fellow-team members are best supported in a physical Obeya, where we can experience seeing, learning and acting together in one big room.

[*] Alpha type comes from the animal world and refers to the leader of a group who gets to be the leader by being dominant above others. In this context, alpha leaders are not physically but verbally dominant, opinionated and use punishment (anger) and reward behaviors of others.

When we stand in one room together, verbal and non-verbal communication and the powerful effect of the visuals on the wall are at their most effective. This is where the magic happens in the Obeya.

But what to do when standing in the same room together is not an option?

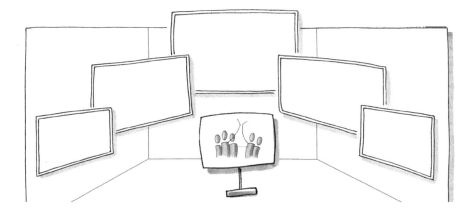

We should distinguish three forms of Obeya when it comes to virtualization and team interaction:

Local – A physical room in one location where the leadership team meets in person. Information may be presented physically or digitally through screens (though the first has the preference).

Hybrid – People either meet in the room or from a remote location via video conference. The physical room may be accessed via that video conference, or it may be mirrored virtually and/or physically on another location. In order for remote participants to view and interact with the information on the wall, a central (digital) repository of the information, or a virtual version of the Obeya is created that looks just like the real one.

Virtual – The room exists only virtually, there is no physical Obeya room, and people participate remotely via video and interactive virtual Obeya tools. Here it is important that the Obeya looks and feels like the original physical Obeya as much as possible. This requires that information from different sources (information systems) is shared on a central 'wall' that is designed for optimum visual flow as described in this book.

Looking at these three options, working in a room physically as a team, interacting with paper content has the preference. People simply bond and interact best when they can be in the same room. In terms of working with information on the walls, the richness of interaction, speed and ease of use with paper and whiteboard walls can be augmented on a screen but it's simply not on the same level (yet).

But you might not have a choice. So if you do shift to hybrid or virtual Obeya, what are things to look out for? Here are some tips:

TIP 1 - MAKE YOUR VIRTUAL OBEYA LOOK LIKE THE REAL ONE USING A CONTEXT SHARING SYSTEM

When you walk into an Obeya, there is a reason why you feel like you're walking into the visual collective mind-space of the leadership team that uses it. You won't get the same feeling when you're looking at a screen at Excel sheets, PowerPoints and portfolio tools. Though essentially the latter may capture and likely be the source of the stuff that you're seeing in the physical Obeya, the magic comes from the way that information is extracted, visualized and placed into context of everything else in the Obeya.

But how do you make your virtual Obeya look like the real one? This can be done using what I'd call a 'Context Sharing System'. Other than 'information systems', which store, process and present specific pieces of information, these Context Sharing Systems are specifically designed with the use of visual management in mind. They start with a blank space, just like a physical whiteboard or a plain white wall. Then the user can add lines, structures, pictures to create the same visual structure as the real Obeya. Adding content is often as easy as dragging and dropping pictures, PDF's or Excel sheets onto the virtual Obeya structure. Lastly, teammates can be added who can update their own information, facilitate sessions and invite guests into the Obeya.

Examples of tools that facilitate context sharing on a whiteboard-like environment are (amongst others) iObeya, Miro, Mural and Nureva.

If you manage to make your virtual and physical Obeya look alike, it will be beneficial to the team as they can rely on their prior knowledge and spatial memory of the Obeya to instantly know where information is placed on the walls. And it will greatly improve the ease of use which promotes adoption of the virtual solution. It maximizes the benefits of using the visual management structure of the Obeya. If your team exists partially or largely of remote participants, creating and maintaining both the virtual and physical Obeya might be worth the effort.

Don't think it will require a lot of time maintaining both a virtual and physical Obeya, as all information is readily present and tracking changes on the Obeya walls - albeit virtual or physical - should largely be done during sessions. They can be captured and managed by a capable facilitator making sure real-time changes are applied both in the physical and virtual Obeya.

TIP 2 – ENSURE GREAT AUDIO AND VIDEO

Trivial as it may seem, having great audio and video in your online sessions really adds value to the team. This is important for two reasons:

1. The more the team is able to see and hear each other in lifelike conditions, the better because it will keep that 'bonding and interaction' intact as much as possible. So create a good setup with proper lighting, a good camera and good sound. The more you can make it look like you're standing next to each other, the better. This effect is often enhanced by 'mirroring', which can be achieved for example when you use the same rooms, layouts on the wall, tables, etc. on both ends of the line. Your screen will 'mirror' your own room, giving the team an enhanced feeling of 'togetherness'.

2. It is important to avoid any distractions in terms of audio and video not related to the Obeya meeting. Any sound, stutter or visual interference of any kind is directly claiming valuable processing power from your brain and everybody else in the meeting. This draining of processing power may be happening under the radar, making you very tired during your online session, or it may be very explicit. For example when you cannot hear each other anymore because there is too much background noise from one of the participants who hasn't put their microphone on mute.

Good use of audio and video boils down two things: (1) people having the right equipment and a suitable physical space to meet online, (2) people are aware of the features of both hardware and software and are capable of using it.

Leadership should invest time and money into providing participants with the right equipment. And they should provide everybody with the basic training in using the functionalities of those tools, to ensure that they are able to participate in the Obeya sessions in best possible way.

TIP 3 – PROVIDE PROPER FACILITATION

Assigning a capable facilitator may even be more important when you're collaborating online. This person certainly should know the ins and outs of the tools you're using to help others. The facilitator can also help setting up and managing meetings with the communications tool and interacting with the information in the Obeya.

With the Context Sharing System we discussed earlier, the facilitator often has extra 'equipment' for facilitation, like timers or the ability to summon all participants to certain areas of the Obeya.

During the meetings, extra effort should be made to ensure that participants are involved, that each participant gets the chance to speak, that actions and decisions are properly put on the designated areas, etc.

Hybrid and virtual Obeyas are taking a giant leap and there will be more developments to come in terms of augmented and virtual reality possibilities. You can follow developments like these and a comparison of tools at ObeyaCoaching.com

Finally, some tips from the trenches

Based on my own experience and conversations with fellow Obeya coaches and leaders, here are a few tips that will help avoid certain pitfalls. Note that many pit falls and tips are already addressed in this book, so this is not a complete list.

ENSURE LEADERSHIP AND EMPLOYEE ENGAGEMENT

The wall must reflect the team's understanding of how their system to achieve the strategic goals works. If the team is not involved, there's no way this is going to happen. Try to facilitate as much co-creation as possible. The same goes for the involvement for the operational teams. If they do their work day-in-day-out, but they cannot relate it to what is in the Obeya of their manager, you've missed the point of cascading.

BUILD TRUST

Leadership teams should pro-actively communicate their intent with adopting Obeya. If there is a lack of trust in the organization, for example, when KPIs have been used as a reward or punish system in the past, then you can be assured teams will look at the Obeya initiative with a healthy dose of suspicion.

The outright aim for the leadership team should be to build trust through transparency. This is probably key to all transformations if you want them to succeed, but particularly so in Lean or Agile transformations which have also been misused for laying off personnel.

CREATE BUY-IN AND DO IT RIGHT THE FIRST TIME

When transforming your way of working to start using Obeya, make sure expectations on what Obeya is are clear. Here you can use the Reference Model to explain the target state for using Obeya with the leadership team so they understand the differences and impact it will have on their current way of working.

They need to be onboard for the full scope. In my experience, starting with a cherry-picking approach (e.g. only implementing the action board first, doing the performance wall after that, etc.) is not productive and will lead to fast decay or complete absence of the effectiveness and promised outcome of working with Obeya.

If you cherry-pick, people will not conceive the full idea of how the Obeya works and will feel the benefits for them are limited. Leading with Obeya as described in this book entails adopting a system. If you pick only one or two components of that system you will find the system is broken.

In one of my own personal experiences, after having launched just the action board in the Obeya on request of the senior leader, one of the managers in the team simply stated after three weeks: "The Obeya isn't working for us, I don't see the added value, we should switch back to the traditional way of running this show."

I realized this manager had no idea what Obeya is, even though everybody had a proper introduction into the concept. After all, in using only the action board we only adopted 1/5 of the visual areas of the Obeya! Before things could get started the concept was declared a failure as far as the manager was concerned and he had a big impact on the team. Bottom-line: be sure the team knows what they're getting themselves into and set expectations for the journey ahead.

ABSORPTION OF INFORMATION BY THE TEAM

The visual management in the Obeya is aimed at supporting the team. At the same time, slapping every piece of information you can find on a wall is of no use to anybody as it becomes an unstructured overkill of information. Information should be coherently consolidated, presented and used in a structured and acceptable way for the team to be able to effectively process it.

The team's ability to consume the available information is always the primary measure for allowance of visuals. I've heard visitors claim about an Obeya that they were visiting that it was just way too complex. But again, as a management team works in the room regularly, their brain familiarizes and as such sees the structure and the logic much more easily.

However, for any new team starting with Obeya the best thing would be to start with the very basic information and build and expand on that as they progress, following an acceptable adoption rate for all members of the team.

BEWARE OF OVER-PRODUCTION

This discussion can lead to super-sized Obeyas with details included from leadership to operational teams. As a result, magnitudes of updating need to happen and instead of creating value, administrative overburden is introduced into the organization. At the same time, teams trying to keep things (too) small may find themselves looking at an updated area in their Obeya and not be able to visually identify problems, their source, or those accountable, and thus not be able to have a productive session as all they can do is guess as to where a problem or potential improvement is actually located.

Selecting the right information depends mostly on the goal, the participants, the context and the next-in-line for your Obeya.

After having baselined the information, as a team grows accustomed to the information on the walls and work with it more, they will also find that they have the mindspace to process more detailed information that will help them reach a meaningful and manageable level at which they can make more impact. This will obviously grow over time, therefore the recommendation is to start at a level at which the team gets an overview of how things are going in relation to their targets, and then use the identification of problems to see if more detailed information is required on their level of visualization.

DISPUTING INFORMATION ON THE WALL

If information on the wall is not updated or there are questions about its correctness, there can be only one course of action to avoid a wasteful conversation in the team: identify the root cause for the late or incorrect report and make sure this is addressed for the next meeting. When information is correct but there are questions that require further digging into the facts to provide a proper answer, then the discussion should be finalized as soon as possible and actions for further clarification on the numbers agreed to. If those actions are registered on the action board the team can follow-up progress before the next meeting.

An important rule to avoid content dispute is to have the content owners place (or at least be responsible to place) the information themselves.

The real challenge is using visuals in such a way that they support the team in a dialogue for grasping their current position on the road to achieving their strategic goals and, of course, uncovering any problems on the way.

AVOID WASTE IN THE OBEYA VISUALS AND ROUTINES

Constantly keeping an eye out on possible waste in the Obeya is a useful recurring exercise. I have witnessed teams repeatedly spend an hour per week updating their portfolio wall, only to not spend one second using or even looking at it during the portfolio wall meeting. Then why update the information at all? In order to avoid the wasteful action of moving non-value add administrative burden from the traditional PPT report to the Obeya wall, let's remember why we are putting information on the wall in the first place:

1. To understand our progress and create context towards our strategic goals and with fellow team members;
2. To identify problems that we must improve in order to better achieve our goals;
3. To learn and improve in being able to achieve our goals.

Once this has been established in the team, the owner of the content must exercise her responsibility to indeed update, improve and represent the information. This can be delegated, but an owner must always be able to explain the story of the visual to the rest of the participants to create context. Failing to do so will result in waste for the meeting and thus for other participants.

The key is finding the right information that truly matters and adds value to the meeting. You will notice this is the case as the information is used to support the context during updates, discussions and, above all, to identify problems. For example, when discussing the impact of a delayed feature or milestone on the change portfolio wall, one would expect the participants to look closer at the wall to identify any consequences the late delivery of that milestone might have for other milestones.

LINK UP WITH YOUR EXISTING GOVERNANCE MODEL TO MAXIMIZE EFFECTIVENESS

The way you govern your organization is related to how you distribute responsibility accountability, and authority. These are distributed in roles, processes, policies and exercised in ad hoc or structural meetings. In the Obeya, on this level your governance model will not change much, though it might become a bit more visible who's responsible for what and who should be in what meeting. But in terms of meeting structure, there will definitely be a few changes. Additionally, you will want to distribute authority in those meetings in such a way that you can make the decisions fast, or get decisions to a level where they can be acted upon quickly.

Appendices

A final word and thanks

This book is my best attempt to translate the things I've learned over the years through reading, experimentation and dialogue with other coaches and users of Obeya into something that will help you look beyond the visuals on the wall of an Obeya.

I hope it has helped you understand what Obeya can do when used for leading organizations. Working with Obeya touches on so many aspects, and we've barely scratched the surface of some of the thinking and techniques I've referred to in this book. I encourage you to be aware of these and to learn, experiment and work on them with your team.

I hope this book has sparked your interest in working with Obeya and maximizing the human leadership potential of your leadership teams. There is so much more to discover in this area and in the many aspects of leadership. I believe we will see many great developments regarding the craft of leadership in the future in relation to Obeya.

If you're inspired to experiment and develop the Obeya concept with your team, and if that helps us move humanity towards the next level by helping leadership create organizations make a better, more responsible impact in this world, then this book has a mission accomplished!

Thanks for those who contributed in one way or the other to this book

I'd like to thank a few others for helping me in the years that I've been working on this book, sometimes even before I was seriously writing. They have helped me develop my understanding of Obeya and leadership, and, therefore, I'd like to thank them for the time we spent together sharing ideas and reflecting on learnings in random order:

Special thanks goes to:

- My parents, Hans and Janny Wiegel for having me over to spend days writing at the house I grew up, and helping me reflect on ideas and improve the reference model.

- Bart Stofberg and Pieter Krop for the fun and valuable learning experiences with Bart's 'Success Breakdown Structure'. Those experiences have been big contributors to the thoughts I'm sharing in this book.

- Koen de Keersmaecker for making the cool drawings in this book and sharing the passion for Obeya.

- David Bogaerts, Liedewij van der Scheer, Paul Wolhoff, Leendert Kalfsbeek, Jannes Smit, Ingeborg ten Berge, Annemiek Quirijns and Nienke Alma for the opportunities at ING Bank to see, learn and act together and do interviews with me.

- Emiel van Est for teaching me about Toyota Kata and the improvement pattern, and for valuable challenges on the ideas in this book.

- Benjamin de Jong and Sytze Hiemstra for sharing their story about the Obeya journey they started in the Summer of 2019 after following the training.

- Sven Dill, Jeroen Venneman for their inspiring words and taking the time to do an interview with me.

- The participants of the Obeya Knowledge Network (meetup & LinkedIn groups) for giving me feedback on the ideas I had for this book.

- Fred Mathyssen for spending time with me sharing his extensive experience with Obeya as a senior leader at Nike and contributing to this book with the interview.

- Steve Bell for reviewing the book and taking the time to correspond and share his views with me. I'd like to specifically thank him for convincing me to relate Obeya more strongly with OKRs, add explicit reference to Hoshin Kanri, and helping me see important aspects of structured problem solving that needed emphasis. Steve's vast knowledge and experience with Lean and specifically also with Obeya have been very helpful and inspiring for some of the paragraphs in this book.

- Laurens Molegraaf, my publisher for moments of reflection and support to get this book where it is today.

- Mieke Storms-Wiegel, my beautiful wife for being eternally patient with me, helping me reflect on the ideas and always be supportive of me and my silly ambition to write a book. She's without a doubt the reason that this book reached the finish line. ;-)

Glossary

Accountability	People (or you) are counting on you to take care of this, it cannot be delegated.
Agile	The Agile values and principles as described in the Agile Manifesto (agilemanifesto.org).
Area	A place where the visuals in the Obeya are placed in such a way that they support the cognitive abilities of the team.
Authority	You can make decisions about something.
Bias	Shortcuts in our brain that help us survive but tend to negatively impact our conscious thinking, learning and ability to make effective decisions.
Cascade	In this book we refer to the cascade as a flow of responsibilities through the organization.
Cognition	Our ability to establish what really happens.
DevOps	A movement of Lean and Agile practitioners that combine the principles and practices with technology and automation, as described in the *DevOps Handbook*.
Governance	The way you have organized leadership in your organization with the distribution of accountability, responsibility and authority.
Heuristics	Thinking pathways that we're likely to take when triggered.

Kata	Derived from martial arts, means "Shape" and is used to teach capabilities. In the Obeya it is used to teach how to work with the information in the areas.
KPI	Key Performance Indicator, a metric with a target or objective, measuring the outcome of something. Unfortunately, it often disregards the way the outcome is established and is regularly tied to personal performance of people and the figure is therefore likely to be manipulated.
Leader	Anybody who feels they have a responsibility to lead other people towards a certain goal. In this book we're looking at the leaders' aspect of leading other people (including oneself), teams and organizations.
Leadership Obeya	Obeya used for leading organizations in the broad sense of the definition (so beyond a single product or project).
Leadership team	The team whose primary goal is to lead the organization (if there is only one team, this is combined with the operational team's responsibilities).
Lean	The interpretation of Toyota's way of working as described by many authors in books as *The Machine That Changed the World*, *The Toyota Way* and *Lean Thinking*.
Metric	Anything that can be measured to study, learn and improve.
Operational team	Teams that do the actual work that adds value for customers.

Outcome Metrics	Measuring the outcome towards a strategic capability or goal. It is a result of underlying elements of your system that you can measure with one or more Supporting Metrics.
Reference Model	Refers to the Leading With Obeya – Reference Model.
Responsibility	You are responsible to care for this in the best way possible, this can be delegated from somebody with the end-accountability.
Scrum	A reference model to adopt Agile ways of working in software development.
Supporting Metrics	These are the metrics we use to expose the parts of the system that help us achieve better outcomes towards strategic capabilities. The Supporting Metrics represent the parts of the system we think we can influence for a better outcome. The outcome is then measured in Outcome Metrics.
Team	Used in this book to indicate the Leadership team.
Transformation Approach	Seven steps that can be combined or spread over time that help transform a team's way of working effectively by avoiding certain pitfalls.
Visual Area(s)	The areas that are visible in the Leading With Obeya – Reference Model.

References / endnotes

1 Toyota (2017). "The Story Behind the Birth of the Prius, Part 2", https://global.toyota/en/detail/20209735

2 Greimel, H. (2012). "Takeshi Uchiyamada helped pilot Toyota through turbulent times", https://www.autonews.com/article/20120521/OEM02/305219959/takeshiuchyamada-helped-pilot-toyota-through-turbulent-times

3 Sutherland, J. (2008). "The First Scrum: Was it Scrum or Lean?", https://www.scruminc.com/is-it-scrum-or-lean/

4 Lamonte, B. & Niven, P. R. (2016). *Objectives and key results: driving focus, alignment, and engagement with OKRs*, John Wiley & Sons, Hoboken, NJ.

5 Wikipedia.org, https://en.wikipedia.org/wiki/Strategy

6 Slightly adapted from: Johnson, S. (2019). "What is the Meaning of Organizational Strategy?", https://smallbusiness.chron.com/meaning-organizational-strategy-59427.html

7 Rigby, D. & B. Bilodeau (2018). "Management Tools & Trends", https://www.bain.com/insights/management-tools-and-trends-2017/

8 Kruse, K. (2012). "What is Employee Engagement", https://www.forbes.com/sites/kevinkruse/2012/06/22/employee-engagement-what-and-why/

9 Beck, R. & J. Harter (2014). "Why Good Managers Are So Rare", https://hbr.org/2014/03/why-good-managers-are-so-rare

10 Wiegel, T.P. (2020). Leadership Systems Survey 2020.

11 *Psychology Today*, https://www.psychologytoday.com/intl/basics/burnout

12 Wiegel, T.P. (2020). Leadership Systems Survey 2020.

13 Kim, G. & P. Debois et al. (2013). *The DevOps Handbook: How to Create World-Class Agility, Reliability, and Security in Technology Organizations*. IT Revolution Press, Portland, OR.

14 Larman, C. "Larman's Law of Organizational Behavior", https://www.craiglarman.com/wiki/index.php?title=Larman%27s_Laws_of_Organizational_Behavior

15 Stofberg, B. (2017). *Iedereen kan innoveren. Stuur op innovatievermogen en niet op innovatie*. Uitgeverij Haystack, Zaltbommel, NL.

16 Taleb, N.N. (2012). *Antifragile: Things That Gain from Disorder*. Random House, New York, NY.

17 Volksgezondheidszorg.info, "Toekomstige trend overspannenheid en burn-out door demografische ontwikkelingen", https://www.volksgezondheidenzorg.info/onderwerp/overspannenheid-en-burn-out/cijfers-context/trends#node-toekomstige-trendoverspannenheid-en-burn-out-door-demografische-ontwikkelingen

18 Robbins, S. & T.A. Judge (2013). *Organizational Behavior*. Pearson, London, UK. p.11, reference 13.

19 Kahneman, D. (2006). *Thinking, Fast and Slow*. Farrar, Straus & Giroux, New York, NY.

20 Benson, B. (2016). "Cognitive bias cheat sheet", https://medium.com/better-humans/cognitive-bias-cheat-sheet-55a472476b18

21 Horgan, S. (2016). "Defeating the Delmore Effect", https://seanhorgan.wordpress.com/2016/10/25/defeating-the-delmore-effect/

22 Wikipedia.org, https://en.wikipedia.org/wiki/Hyperbolic_discounting

23 Kahneman, D. (2006). *Thinking, Fast and Slow*. Farrar, Straus & Giroux, New York, NY.

24 Bocian K. & B. Wojciszke (2014). "Self-Interest Bias in Moral Judgments of Others' Actions", https://journals.sagepub.com/doi/abs/10.1177/0146167214529800

25 DeAngelis, T. (2003). "Why we overestimate our competence", https://www.apa.org/monitor/feb03/overestimate

26 Attolico, L. (2018). *Lean Development and Innovation: Hitting the Market with the Right Products at the Right Time*. Routledge, London, UK.

27 Wikipedia.org, https://en.wikipedia.org/wiki/Motivational_salience

28 Franco-Santos, M. & M. Bourne (2008). "The impact of performance targets on behaviour: A close look at sales force contexts", https://dspace.lib.cranfield.ac.uk/bitstream/handle/1826/4222/Impact_of_performance_targets_on_behaviour.pdf;sequence=1

29 Franco-Santos, M. & M. Bourne (2008). "The impact of performance targets on behaviour: A close look at sales force contexts", https://dspace.lib.cranfield.ac.uk/bitstream/handle/1826/4222/Impact_of_performance_targets_on_behaviour.pdf;sequence=1

30 Haslam, S.A., S.D. Reicher & M.J. Platow (2010). *The New Psychology of Leadership: Identity, Influence and Power*. Psychology Press, London, UK.

31 Haslam, S.A., S.D. Reicher & M.J. Platow (2010). *The New Psychology of Leadership: Identity, Influence and Power*. Psychology Press, London, UK.

32 Robbins, S. & T.A. Judge (2013). *Organizational Behavior*. Pearson, London, UK.

33 Wiegel, T.P. (2020). Leadership Systems Survey 2020.

34 Gharajedaghi, J. (2006) *Systems Thinking: Managing Chaos and Complexity: A Platform for Designing Business Architecture*. Morgan Kaufmann, Burlington, MA.

35 Hutchins, D. (2008), *Hoshin Kanri, The Strategic Approach to Continuous Improvement*, Routledge, London, UK.

36 Taleb, N.N. (2012). *Antifragile: Things That Gain from Disorder*. Random House, New York, NY.

37 Elmansy, R. (2017). "How to Create the Systems Thinking Diagrams", https://www.designorate.com/system-thinking-diagrams/

38 Witten, I.B. & E.I. Knudsen (2005). "Why Seeing is Believing: Merging Auditory and Visual Worlds", https://www.cell.com/neuron/fulltext/S0896-6273(05)00885-8

39 Wikipedia.org, https://en.wikipedia.org/wiki/Visual_system

40 Robbins, S. & T.A. Judge (2013). *Organizational Behavior*. Pearson, London, UK.

41 Robbins, S. & T.A. Judge (2013). *Organizational Behavior*. Pearson, London, UK.

42 Todd, J.J. & R. Marois (2004). "Capacity limit of visual short-term memory in human posterior parietal cortex", https://www.nature.com/articles/nature02466

43 Masai, P. (2017). "Modelling the Lean organization as a complex system. Computational Complexity".

44 Rother, M. (2009). *Toyota Kata*. McGraw-Hill, New York, NY.

45 Gladwell, M. (2018). "Malcolm Gladwell Demystifies 10,000 Hours Rule", https://www.youtube.com/watch?v=1uB5PUpGzeY

46 Liker, J.T. (2004). *The Toyota Way, 14 Management Principles from the World's Greatest Manufacturer*. McGraw-Hill, New York, NY.

47 Kahneman, D. (2006). *Thinking, Fast and Slow*. Farrar, Straus & Giroux, New York, NY.

48 Sutherland, J. & B. Bennett (2007). *The Seven Deadly Wastes of Logistics: Applying Toyota Production System Principles to Create Logistics Value*.

49 Taylor, F.W. (1911). *The Principles of Scientific Management*. Harper & Brothers, New York/London.

50 Deming, W.E. (1993). *The New Economics for Industry, Government, and Education*. MIT Press, Cambridge, MA. p.135.

51 Chakravorty, S.S. (2010). "Where Process-Improvement Projects Go Wrong", https://www.wsj.com/articles/SB10001424052748703298004574457471313938130

52 Shook, J. (2008) *Managing to Learn: Using the A3 Management Process to Solve Problems, Gain Agreement, Mentor and Lead*, Lean Enterprise Institute US, Boston, MA.

53 Rother, M. (2009). *Toyota Kata*. McGraw-Hill, New York, NY. p.17-18

54 devopsdays Detroit (2017), September 28

55 Marquet, L.D. (2013). *Turn the Ship Around!: A True Story of Turning Followers into Leaders*. Portfolio, New York, NY.

56 McDermott, R. (1980). "Profile: Ray L. Birdwhistell", *Kinesis report*, v.2, no.3.

57 Greimel, H. (2012). "Takeshi Uchiyamada helped pilot Toyota through turbulent times", https://www.autonews.com/article/20120521/OEM02/305219959/takeshiuchiyamada-helped-pilot-toyota-through-turbulent-times

58 Buckingham, M. (1999). *First, Break All The Rules: What the World's Greatest Managers Do Differently*. Gallup Press, Princeton, NJ.

59 Sinek, S. (2009). *Start with Why: How Great Leaders Inspire Everyone to Take Action*. Penguin Random House, New York, NY.

60 Lencioni, P. (2002). *The Five Dysfunctions of a Team: A Leadership Fable*. Jossey-Bass, Hoboken, NJ.

61 Johnson, G., K. Scholes & R. Whittington (2009). *Fundamentals of Strategy with MyStrategyLab*. Prentice Hall, Upper Saddle River, NJ.

62 Kniberg, H. & Ivarsson, A., 2012, 'Scaling Agile @ Spotify with Tribes, Squads, Chapters & Guilds', blog.crisp.se

63 Department of Trade and Industry (2015). "Achieving Best Practice in Your Business: Quality, cost, delivery: measuring business performance", https://www.industryforum. co.uk/wp-content/uploads/sites/6/2015/07/QCD.pdf

64 Deming, W.E. (1993). *The New Economics for Industry, Government, and Education*. MIT Press, Cambridge, MA. p.135.

65 Ridgway, V.F. (1956). "Dysfunctional Consequences of Performance Measurements", *Administrative Science Quarterly*, vol.1, no.2, p.240-247.

66 Ries, E. (2013). *The Lean Startup: How Today's Entrepreneurs Use Continuous Innovation to Create Radically Successful Businesses*. Currency, New York, NY.

67 Shook, J. (2008), *Managing to learn: using the a3 management process to solve problems, gain agreement, mentor & lead*, Lean Enterprise Institute US, Boston, MA.

68 Pink, D. (2009). *Drive: The Surprising Truth About What Motivates Us*. Riverhead Books, New York, NY.

69 Kahneman, D. (2006). *Thinking, Fast and Slow*. Farrar, Straus & Giroux, New York, NY.

About the Author

Tim Wiegel is a dedicated Obeya coach who has witnessed firsthand the breakthrough changes within teams, when strategy leads to meaningful action and performance.

He has over ten years of coaching and consulting experience, working at banks, public services, healthcare, government, industry and telco companies. Recognizing there was a deeper problem to many of the projects he was asked to do, he started his learning journey on Lean and Agile ways of working in 2012. But things really clicked when he learned about Obeya at the 2014 Lean IT Summit in Paris. Since then, he studied, experimented and helped teams get started with Obeya, from start-ups to boardrooms.

Tim has witnessed many teams make a remarkable claim: "Now we cannot imagine how we used to manage our organization without Obeya". Leading with Obeya builds upon the broad spectrum of experiences and learnings throughout Tim's career, providing a common-sense approach for leadership teams to make a difference in this world.

Tim leads up a coaching network that provides training and coaching at ObeyaCoaching.com and drives a growing community of people interested to lead their organization with Obeya.